FITWAFFLE'S

EASY

6

Eloise Head

hamlyn

Contents

ABOUT ME   4

ABOUT THE BOOK   6

THE STAPLE SIX   8

TIPS & TRICKS   10

CHAPTER 1: BREAKFAST   12

CHAPTER 2: LUNCH   42

CHAPTER 3: PASTA & NOODLES   70

CHAPTER 4: DINNER   100

CHAPTER 5: SNACKS & SIDES   124

CHAPTER 6: BAKES & CAKES   146

CHAPTER 7: NO-BAKE DESSERTS   182

INDEX   220

GLOSSARY OF UK/US TERMS   222

ACKNOWLEDGEMENTS   223

About Me

Hi, I'm Eloise, though most people online know me as Fitwaffle.

I spend my days developing recipes, creating food videos for people all over social media and writing cookbooks (which still feels a bit surreal to say out loud). I'm a proud foodie, a bestselling author and, once upon a time, a personal trainer.

People often ask me where the name Fitwaffle came from. It actually started years ago when I was working full time in the fitness industry. Back then, I was learning how to enjoy food in a balanced way after struggling with a pretty negative relationship with it. I wanted a name that brought together both my passions – fitness and food. As well as fitness, the 'fit' part is also about fitting all foods into your diet. And the 'waffle' part? Well, that's partly about my love of waffles and desserts, but also because I'm known to talk a little (okay, a lot).

My love of food goes way back to childhood. I used to bake with my Great Auntie Pearl, who was a huge influence on me. We would spend hours in the kitchen making biscuits, cakes and all sorts of pastry creations. Looking back, those moments were when my passion for baking really began. She also made roast potatoes that, to this day, no one else has managed to better.

These days, my mission is simple. I want to help people feel more confident in the kitchen and show that baking and cooking don't need to be complicated or scary. Whether you're brand new in the kitchen or you've been doing it for years, my goal is to share recipes that are fun, straightforward and completely doable, no matter your skill level.

So, that's me in a nutshell. Now let's get to the good part...the food!

Eloise
x

About the Book

These are quick, flavoursome and fuss-free recipes for real life.

I'm so excited about this book, because honestly, it's the book I wish I'd written sooner.

Like so many people, I know what it's like to feel too tired or too busy to cook. Cooking can feel stressful. You're staring into the fridge, you don't know what to make, or you've found a recipe that looks amazing...until you see the 20 ingredients it needs. And sometimes, it just feels way easier to throw a ready meal in the oven (been there, done that, many times).

That's why I wanted to create this. A book that makes cooking and baking easier, quicker and actually enjoyable. Every recipe uses no more than six main ingredients (plus a few staples you'll already have at home), so there's less fuss, less time in the kitchen and less overwhelm.

Most of the recipes are ready in under 30 minutes, and there's a mix of everyday savoury dishes – like pastas, salads, tacos and more – and of course the fun bakes too. Because for me, it's all about balance: food that's nourishing and flavoursome, but also comforting and fun. Food that keeps your body feeling good and also your mind.

Who's it for?

This book is for you if you:

- Get overwhelmed by complicated recipes
- Don't want to spend hours in the kitchen
- Are a student, a beginner or a busy parent
- Or just want tasty food without the faff.

How it works

The recipes taste amazing exactly as they are, but they're also flexible. Think of them as go-to recipes that you can add your own twist to if you want.

I really hope this book helps you fall in love with cooking and baking, and shows you that it doesn't have to be complicated to taste amazing.

The Staple Six

Here are the six staple ingredients we will use throughout the book, which won't be counted as part of the six main ingredients in the recipes. These are everyday ingredients that you probably already have in your cupboard, and that also have a long shelf-life. I've labelled these as 'Staple Ingredients', and you'll see these listed under the main ingredients list on each recipe page.

1 Salt

Salt is a foundational seasoning in cooking. It enhances the natural flavours of ingredients, balances sweetness or bitterness and can also be used to preserve food. You'll see salt pop up a lot in this book.

2 Pepper

Pepper adds a mild heat and depth of flavour to dishes. We'll pair this often with salt to season the food.

3 Oil for savoury dishes, such as olive

Oil is a kitchen staple for cooking, frying, roasting and making dressings or marinades. It helps conduct heat, prevents food from sticking, adds richness and can improve texture. I usually reach for olive oil when I'm cooking savoury dishes, but you can use whatever you prefer and already keep in your kitchen.

4 Neutral oil for baking, such as rapeseed

When it comes to baking, you'll want a neutral, almost flavourless oil so it doesn't overpower the taste of your cake or dessert. I like using rapeseed (canola) oil, but sunflower or vegetable oil also work well.

5 Paprika

Paprika is a ground spice made from dried red peppers. It adds colour, mild sweetness or smokiness (depending on whether it is sweet paprika or smoked paprika) and a warm flavour to dishes. It's one of my favourite base seasonings.

6 Cayenne pepper

Cayenne pepper is a ground chilli powder and brings intense heat and a sharp, pungent spice to food. A little goes a long way.

Tips & Tricks

Portions
Most of the savoury recipes in this book are designed to serve 1 or 2, but you can easily double or even triple the recipe to feed a family or batch cook so you have leftovers for the next day.

Freezer-friendly
When baking or cooking in batches, you can always freeze the extra portions for another day. Make sure you let the food cool down fully, then portion it up, wrap it well so no moisture can get it, stick a label on it so you know when it was made and what it is, then freeze it straight away. Thaw it in the fridge before use and reheat as normal.

Unapologetic shortcuts
Don't be afraid to make it easy for yourself. Ingredients such as garlic purée, ready-rolled pastry, spice blends, pesto, ready-made caramel, cooking sauces and frozen alternatives can save time, effort and even money.

Ingredient swaps
If you don't have a particular ingredient to hand, don't stress. In many recipes you can swap like for like. For example, use milk chocolate chips instead of dark, spinach instead of kale, or try a different type of nut. Feel free to add extra seasonings or swap in your favourites. I'll highlight where swaps and add-ins work best, but don't be afraid to adapt to what you have at home.

Equipment
I've kept the equipment as simple as possible – just a couple of different sizes of saucepan and a large nonstick frying pan, some ovenproof dishes and standard baking tins for the sweet stuff. Especially when it comes to baking, stick to the tin or dish size specified as best as possible, otherwise it may not cook properly. I'd also recommend an electric hand mixer to speed up whipping cream!

Ovens and air fryers
Remember that all ovens and air fryers vary slightly, so keep an eye on your food (especially when baking) towards the end of the cooking time. If something looks ready early, trust your instincts, and if it needs a few extra minutes, that's perfectly normal too.

This book doesn't require an air fryer, but if you have one don't be afraid to use it. It's perfect for cooking up smaller portions or side dishes. Even if the recipe states to use an oven, if it fits in the air fryer, go for it! As a rough guide, convert the oven instructions to air fryer by turning the temperature down by 20°C (68°F) and reducing the cooking time by 20 per cent.

Cleaning and care
Line your tins and trays with baking paper whenever you can. It makes removing food easier and washing up much quicker.

Breakfast

VEGGIE BREAKFAST BUN 14

E.A.T. BREAKFAST BAGEL 16

CHEESE & RED PEPPER EGG BITES 18

CREAMY AVOCADO TOAST 20

ULTIMATE BREAKFAST SANDWICH 22

NUTTY GRANOLA BARS 24

BROWNIE BAKED OATS 26

BLUEBERRY MUFFIN BAKED OATS 28

SALTED CARAMEL GRANOLA 30

BLUEBERRY CHEESECAKE OVERNIGHT OATS 32

TROPICAL BLISS SMOOTHIE BOWL 34

SPECULOOS FRENCH TOAST STICKS 36

EVERYDAY PROTEIN PANCAKES 38

RASPBERRY RIPPLE CHIA PUDDING 40

Veggie Breakfast Bun

This soft bun is loaded with egg, cheese, hash browns and tomatoes. It's quick to make, super satisfying and easy to customize with whatever you've got in the fridge.

INGREDIENTS:

2 frozen hash browns

1 brioche bun or soft sandwich roll

1 egg

1 tablespoon sauce, such as mayo or ketchup

1 slice of tomato, or a few thin slices

1 slice of Cheddar or American cheese

STAPLE INGREDIENTS:

Salt

Pepper

Olive oil

1 Cook the hash browns according to packet instructions. I like to cook mine in the air fryer at 200°C (400°F) for 12–15 minutes, flipping halfway.

2 While the hash browns cook, split the bun and lightly toast the cut sides in a dry frying pan, then set aside.

3 Heat a little oil in a nonstick frying pan over a medium-high heat. Crack in the egg, season with salt and pepper, and fry to your liking. I like to flip mine once the edges and base are crisp.

4 Spread the sauce on the bottom half of the bun and add the slice(s) of tomato.

5 Pile the hash browns on top, followed by the slice of cheese and the fried egg. The heat from the hash browns and the egg will gently melt the cheese.

6 Place the bun lid on top and serve (be careful, the hash browns will be very hot).

TIPS

Feel free to sprinkle with chopped chives, paprika or cayenne pepper for some extra smokiness or a little kick.

Add a blob of my Everything Sauce on page 66 for extra deliciousness!

E.A.T. Breakfast Bagel
(Egg, Avocado, Tomato)

Egg, avocado and tomato all tucked inside a chewy bagel. Simple, fresh and so good, it's the kind of breakfast that feels special but only takes a few minutes to put together.

INGREDIENTS:

1 bagel

1 egg

½ avocado

1 slice of tomato, or a few thin slices

1 slice of Cheddar or American cheese

Handful of spinach or rocket

STAPLE INGREDIENTS:

Salt

Pepper

Olive oil

Paprika (optional)

1 Split and toast the bagel until golden and lightly crisp.

2 While the bagel is toasting, heat a little oil in a nonstick frying pan over a medium-high heat. Crack in the egg, season with salt and pepper, and fry to your liking. I like to flip mine once the edges and base are crisp.

3 Slice or mash the avocado. Season with salt and pepper and a pinch of paprika if you like.

4 Spread the avocado over the bottom half of the bagel.

5 Layer on the tomato, fried egg, cheese and spinach or rocket.

6 Place the other half of the bagel on top and serve warm.

TIP

Add a spoon of spicy mayo or Everything Sauce (see page 66) for extra flavour!

Cheese & Red Pepper Egg Bites

These fluffy little egg bites are packed with roasted red pepper and gooey cheese. They're great for breakfast on the go or a quick snack any time of the day.

INGREDIENTS:

4 large eggs

2½ tablespoons Greek yogurt

60g (2¼oz) Cheddar cheese, grated

½ red pepper, cored, deseeded and finely diced

1 spring onion, finely sliced

STAPLE INGREDIENTS:

Salt

Pepper

Olive oil

Paprika

1   Preheat your oven to 190°C, 170°C fan (375°F), Gas Mark 5 and lightly grease 6 holes of a muffin tin with oil or line with muffin cases.

2   In a bowl or jug, whisk together the eggs, Greek yogurt, ¼ teaspoon of paprika and a pinch of salt and pepper until combined.

3   Stir in the grated cheese, red pepper and spring onion and divide the mixture between the 6 muffin holes, filling each about three-quarters full.

4   Place the muffin tin in a large roasting tin. Carefully pour hot water into the roasting tin, about halfway up the sides. This creates a simple water bath, which helps the egg cook gently and stay soft.

5   Bake for 20–25 minutes or until the bites are just set in the centre and slightly puffed. Let them cool for 5 minutes before removing from the tin. Enjoy hot or cold.

6   Store in an airtight container in the refrigerator for up to 4 days. To reheat, place 1 or 2 in the microwave and heat on low-medium power for 30–45 seconds or until warmed through. Avoid high power, as this can make them rubbery.

Creamy Avocado Toast

Smooth, creamy avocado spread over crispy toast – this is a classic for a reason.
Here it's topped with a drizzle of hot honey for the ultimate sweet and savoury combo.

INGREDIENTS:

1 slice of sourdough bread

1 small avocado, halved

½ garlic clove or ½ teaspoon
   garlic purée

3½ tablespoons Greek yogurt

Juice of ½ lemon

Hot honey, to drizzle

STAPLE INGREDIENTS:

Salt

Pepper

1   Toast the sourdough slice until golden and crisp.

2   While the bread is toasting, scoop the avocado flesh into a blender or food processor with the garlic, Greek yogurt, lemon juice and a pinch of salt and pepper. Blend for 20–30 seconds until smooth and creamy.

   If you don't have a blender, mash the avocado well with a fork. Finely grate or mince the garlic if using fresh, then stir it into the avocado with the yogurt, lemon juice, salt and pepper. Mix vigorously until as smooth and whipped as possible.

3   Spread the creamy avocado mixture over the toasted sourdough.

4   Drizzle with hot honey and serve straight away. If you like, add an extra sprinkle of pepper.

TIP

You could also top
the avocado toast
with a pinch of chilli
flakes or flaky salt.

Ultimate Breakfast Sandwich

This is everything you could want in a breakfast bun – eggs, bacon, sausage, cheese and sauce piled into one epic sandwich. Perfect for those mornings you need something filling enough to keep you going for hours.

INGREDIENTS:

1 brioche bun or soft sandwich roll

1 sausage patty or 2 sausages, skinned and shaped

2 slices of bacon or turkey bacon

1 egg

1 tablespoon sauce, such as mayo or ketchup

1 slice of Cheddar or American cheese

STAPLE INGREDIENTS:

Salt

Pepper

Olive oil

1 Split the bun and lightly toast the cut sides in a dry frying pan, then set aside.

2 Heat a little oil in a large frying pan over a medium heat. Cook the sausage patty for 2–3 minutes per side until browned and cooked through. At the same time, fry the bacon until crispy or to your liking.

3 Crack the egg into the pan, season with salt and pepper, and fry to your liking. I like to flip mine once the edges and base are crisp.

4 Spread the sauce on the bottom half of the bun, then layer on the sausage patty, cheese, bacon and egg.

5 Place the bun lid on top and serve straight away.

TIPS

For extra flavour, mix mayo and ketchup together or use a spoonful of my Everything Sauce on page 66.

Feel free to add a sprinkle of chopped chives for extra colour and flavour.

Nutty Granola Bars

Chewy, crunchy and loaded with nuts, these granola bars are perfect for keeping in your bag for a quick pick-me-up. They're simple, satisfying and so much tastier than shop-bought bars.

INGREDIENTS:

100g (3½oz) honey or maple syrup

90g (3¼oz) smooth peanut or almond butter

1 teaspoon vanilla extract

90g (3¼oz) rolled oats

125g (4½oz) mixed nuts, such as almonds, cashews and hazelnuts, roughly chopped

80g (2¾oz) dried fruit, such as raisins, cranberries and chopped apricots

STAPLE INGREDIENTS:

Salt

1 Preheat your oven to 180°C, 160°C fan (350°F), Gas Mark 4 and line a 20cm (8 inch) square tin with baking paper, leaving some overhang for easy removal.

2 In a saucepan over a low heat, melt the honey and peanut butter, and stir together until smooth and combined. Remove from the heat and stir in the vanilla extract and ¼ teaspoon of salt.

3 Tip the oats, nuts and dried fruit into the pan and stir to combine.

4 Tip the mixture into your prepared tin and press firmly into an even layer using the back of a spoon.

5 Bake in the oven for 15–18 minutes until golden around the edges. Allow to cool completely in the tin before slicing into 8 bars.

6 Store in an airtight container for up to 5 days or in the refrigerator for up to 2 weeks. You can also freeze the bars for up to 2 months.

Brownie Baked Oats

All the flavour of a gooey chocolate brownie, but in oat form.
Warm, rich and filling – perfect if you love chocolate!

INGREDIENTS:

½ large banana (about 50g/1¾oz
    peeled weight)

1 egg

4 tablespoons milk (any)

50g (1¾oz) rolled oats

½ teaspoon baking powder

1 tablespoon cocoa powder

STAPLE INGREDIENTS:

Salt

1 Preheat your oven to 180°C, 160°C fan (350°F), Gas Mark 4 and lightly grease 2 ovenproof ramekins or an ovenproof dish, 8–10cm (3¼–4 inches) in diameter.

2 In a bowl, mash the banana until smooth. Add the egg and milk, and mix well until combined.

3 Add the oats, baking powder, cocoa powder and a pinch of salt, and mix until smooth.

4 Pour the mixture into your prepared ramekins or dish and bake for 20 minutes or until set in the middle, but still soft. Don't overbake otherwise it can become dry.

5 Leave to stand for a few minutes before serving. Be careful, as the dish will be very hot.

TIPS

For a cakier texture, blend the oats to a powder first.

If you like, add 20g (¾oz) of chocolate chips or chunks to the mixture before pouring into the dish.

Blueberry Muffin Baked Oats

These oats taste just like a blueberry muffin straight from the oven. They're sweet, fruity and guaranteed to brighten up your morning.

INGREDIENTS:

50g (1¾oz) rolled oats

4 tablespoons Greek or plain yogurt

30ml (1fl oz) honey or maple syrup

10g (¼oz) unsalted butter, melted and cooled slightly

4 tablespoons milk (any)

Handful of fresh blueberries

STAPLE INGREDIENTS:

Salt

1 Preheat your oven to 200°C, 180°C fan (400°F), Gas Mark 6 and lightly grease 2 ovenproof ramekins or an ovenproof dish, 8–10cm (3¼–4 inches) in diameter.

2 In a small bowl, combine the oats, yogurt, honey, melted butter, milk and a pinch of salt. Mix until full combined.

3 Gently fold in most of the blueberries, keeping some aside.

4 Pour the mixture into the prepared ramekins or dish, then scatter the remaining blueberries on top.

5 Bake for 20–25 minutes until cooked through and lightly golden. The cooking time will vary depending on the size of your dish.

6 Leave to stand for a few minutes before serving. Be careful, as the dish will be very hot.

TIP

For a cakier texture, blend the oats to a powder first.

Salted Caramel Granola

These crunchy oat clusters have a sweet-salty caramel twist.
Sprinkle over yogurt, enjoy with milk or just eat by the handful.

INGREDIENTS:

250g (9oz) rolled oats
80g (2¾oz) light soft brown sugar
1 teaspoon sea salt flakes
100ml (3½fl oz) honey or maple syrup
2 teaspoons vanilla extract

STAPLE INGREDIENTS:

Neutral oil, such as rapeseed

1 Preheat your oven to 180°C, 160°C fan (350°F), Gas Mark 4 and line a large baking tray with baking paper.

2 In a large mixing bowl, combine the oats, sugar and sea salt. Stir to mix evenly.

3 In a small saucepan over a low heat, warm the honey, vanilla extract and 4 tablespoons of oil until runny and well combined (do not boil).

4 Pour the wet mixture over the oat mixture and stir well until everything is fully coated.

5 Spread the granola mixture out evenly on the prepared tray, pressing down gently with the back of a spoon to encourage clusters.

6 Bake for 20–25 minutes, stirring halfway, until golden and fragrant. Keep an eye on it in the last few minutes to prevent burning.

7 Remove from the oven and leave to cool completely – it will crisp up as it cools. Store in an airtight container for up to 2 weeks.

TIP

Stir 50g (1¾oz) dark or milk chocolate chips into the granola after it has cooled if you like.

Blueberry Cheesecake Overnight Oats

These creamy overnight oats are layered with juicy blueberries.
They're fruity, indulgent and taste like dessert for breakfast.

INGREDIENTS:

50g (1¾oz) rolled oats

75ml (2½fl oz) Greek yogurt

1–3 teaspoons honey or maple syrup

½ teaspoon vanilla extract

125ml (4fl oz) milk (any)

Handful of fresh or frozen blueberries

1 In a small bowl or jar, combine the oats, Greek yogurt, honey to taste, vanilla extract and milk. Stir until everything is fully mixed and creamy.

2 Fold in the blueberries (if using frozen, they'll thaw overnight and add a gorgeous purple colour). Stir gently to distribute evenly.

3 Cover and chill in the refrigerator for at least 4 hours or ideally overnight to allow the oats to soak and soften.

4 In the morning, give it a stir and enjoy.

TIP

For an extra cheesecake feel, top with crushed digestive biscuits in the morning before you tuck in.

Tropical Bliss Smoothie Bowl

This sunshine-filled bowl is fresh, vibrant and guaranteed to give you summer vibes any time of the year. Try out different toppings to keep breakfast interesting.

INGREDIENTS:

150g (5½oz) frozen mango chunks

150g (5½oz) frozen pineapple chunks

100ml (3½fl oz) Greek or plain yogurt

1 tablespoon honey or maple syrup (optional)

2 tablespoons milk (any)

1 Place the frozen mango and pineapple, yogurt, honey, if using, and milk in a high-speed blender.

2 Blend on high until completely smooth and thick. Scrape down the sides and stir if needed to keep things moving. You want a scoopable texture, not a drinkable one.

3 Transfer to a chilled bowl and serve straight away.

TIP

Add toppings to your smoothie bowl, if you like. I like sliced kiwi, toasted coconut flakes and granola, but sliced mango and pineapple or chia seeds work well too.

Speculoos French Toast Sticks

Crispy golden French toast is filled with gooey Biscoff spread. It's fun to eat, perfect for dipping and guaranteed to please any Biscoff lover!

INGREDIENTS:

4 slices of soft thick-cut white bread

2–3 tablespoons Biscoff spread

1 large egg

4 tablespoons milk (any)

2 tablespoons granulated sugar

1 teaspoon ground cinnamon

STAPLE INGREDIENTS:

Neutral oil, such as rapeseed

1 Lay the slices of bread on a board and remove the crusts if desired.

2 Spread the Biscoff spread over 2 slices of the bread, then top with the other 2 slices to make sandwiches.

3 Slice each sandwich into 3 even sticks.

4 In a shallow bowl, whisk together the egg and milk until well combined. Heat a little oil in a large frying pan over a medium heat.

5 Dip each stick into the egg mixture, turning to coat (you don't need to soak them), then transfer to the hot pan.

6 Cook for 1–2 minutes on each side until golden brown.

7 While they're cooking, mix the sugar and cinnamon together in a shallow bowl or on a plate. Once the French toast sticks are cooked, immediately roll them in the cinnamon sugar to coat them. Serve straight away while still warm.

Everyday Protein Pancakes

These fluffy pancakes are made with everyday ingredients – no protein powder required. They're light yet satisfying, and taste amazing with any of your favourite toppings.

INGREDIENTS:

40g (1½oz) oat flour or rolled oats

100ml (3½fl oz) Greek yogurt

1 egg

1 teaspoon vanilla extract

Pinch of ground cinnamon (optional)

Small handful of white chocolate chips (optional)

STAPLE INGREDIENTS:

Neutral oil, such as rapeseed

1 If you're starting with rolled oats, blitz them in a blender or crush them in your fingers until you have a fairly fine flour.

2 In a bowl, whisk together the Greek yogurt, egg and vanilla extract until smooth.

3 Add the oat flour and mix until just combined. The batter should be super thick. If using cinnamon or chocolate chips, mix them in now.

4 Heat a nonstick frying pan over a medium heat and lightly grease it with oil.

5 Spoon the batter into the pan, about 2 tablespoons per pancake, to make 3 small pancakes. Spread the batter out with the back of a spoon if needed.

6 Cook for 2–3 minutes until the edges are golden and they hold their shape enough to flip. Cook on the other side for 1–2 minutes until golden and cooked through.

7 Serve warm with your favourite toppings.

TIP

You can add any of your favourite toppings to these pancakes. I like a scoop of Greek yogurt, with blueberries, maple syrup or honey and a few white chocolate chips.

Raspberry Ripple Chia Pudding

This creamy chia pudding is swirled with raspberries for a fruity ripple effect. Light, refreshing and great as a make-ahead breakfast or snack.

INGREDIENTS:

3 tablespoons chia seeds

200ml (7fl oz) milk (any)

3½ tablespoons Greek yogurt

½ teaspoon vanilla extract

2 tablespoons fresh or frozen raspberries, plus extra to serve

1 tablespoon granola, or ½ digestive biscuit, crushed

1   In a jar or bowl, mix the chia seeds with the milk, Greek yogurt and vanilla extract until well combined, then fold in the raspberries.

2   Leave to rest for 5 minutes, then stir again to prevent clumping.

3   Cover and chill in the refrigerator for at least 2 hours or overnight.

4   Stir well before serving, topped with the granola or crushed biscuit, and a few extra raspberries if you like.

TIPS

If you like things sweeter, you can stir in a little honey or maple syrup in Step 1.

For an ultra-smooth version, blend the pudding after setting, then add your toppings.

Lunch

CRISPY CHICKEN CAESAR SANDWICH 44

BEST EVER GRILLED CHEESE 46

TOMATO & BUTTER BEAN SOUP 48

VEGGIE BURRITO BOWL 50

FANCY PIZZA TOAST 52

SWEET CHILLI CHICKEN WRAP 54

AUTUMN HARVEST SALAD / HONEY MUSTARD VINAIGRETTE 56

PIZZA SALAD / CREAMY AVOCADO SALAD 57

CRUNCHY RAINBOW WRAP 60

CHEESE & HAM TOASTIE DIPPERS 62

MEXICAN-STYLE CHICKEN & SWEETCORN SOUP 64

CHEESEBURGER BOWL / EVERYTHING SAUCE 66

CHICKEN AVOCADO BURRITO 68

Crispy Chicken Caesar Sandwich

Take everything you love about a Caesar salad – crunchy chicken, crisp lettuce, creamy dressing – and put it in bread! This is a sandwich you'll keep coming back to.

INGREDIENTS:

2 chicken breasts

60g (2¼oz) cornflakes

1 large egg, beaten

2 long rolls (ideally brioche)

125ml (4fl oz) Caesar dressing

2 handfuls of iceberg lettuce, chopped

STAPLE INGREDIENTS:

Salt

Pepper

Paprika

TIP

Add a sprinkle of grated Parmesan cheese on top of the lettuce before closing the sandwiches for extra flavour.

1 If cooking the chicken in the oven, preheat to 220°C, 200°C fan (425°F), Gas Mark 7 and line a baking tray with foil.

2 Place the chicken breasts between 2 sheets of baking paper and tenderize (flatten) them using a meat mallet or the base of a saucepan – this will help them cook more evenly and improve the texture. Season on both sides with salt, pepper and paprika.

3 Put the cornflakes into a food processor and process until roughly crushed. Alternatively, put them into a plastic bag and crush with a rolling pin, then pour into a bowl.

4 Coat the chicken in the egg, letting any excess drip off, then in the crushed cornflakes, making sure you pat them really firmly on both sides of the chicken.

5 Transfer the coated chicken breasts to your foil-lined tray if baking in the oven, or to your air fryer basket, making sure they're not touching each other. Air fry at 180°C (350°F) for 12–14 minutes, or cook in the oven for 20–22 minutes, until the chicken is cooked through and at least 75°C (167°F) when tested with a meat thermometer.

6 While they're cooking, split the rolls and lightly toast the cut sides in a dry frying pan, then set aside.

7 Spread some Caesar dressing over the bottom half of each roll. Put the remaining Caesar dressing in a bowl, then add the chopped lettuce and toss to coat it well.

8 Place a cooked chicken breast on the bottom half of each roll, then place the Caesar lettuce on top, followed by the other half of each roll and close the sandwiches.

Best Ever Grilled Cheese

Sometimes simple is best, and this grilled cheese proves it. Crispy, buttery bread oozes with gooey melted cheese and caramelized onion jam. Perfection!

INGREDIENTS:

1 teaspoon mayonnaise

1 teaspoon yellow mustard

2 slices of thick-cut white bread or sourdough

1 tablespoon caramelized onion jam or chutney

60g (2¼oz) Cheddar cheese, grated

½ tablespoon butter, softened, plus extra for frying (optional)

STAPLE INGREDIENTS:

Pepper (optional)

Olive oil

1 In a small bowl, mix the mayonnaise and mustard together and spread on one of the slices of bread.

2 Spread the caramelized onion jam over the mustard-mayo layer, then top with grated cheese. Season with black pepper if you like.

3 Place the other slice of bread on top, then butter the outsides of the sandwich.

4 Heat a nonstick frying pan over medium-low heat and add a little drizzle of oil or butter.

5 Fry the sandwich for 3–4 minutes on each side, pressing them down gently with a spatula until the bread is golden and crisp, and the cheese has melted.

6 Slice in half and serve hot. Enjoy!

TIP

If you prefer, use a mixture of grated Cheddar and mozzarella for a really stretchy filling.

Serves 2–4 · Prep time: 5 minutes · Cooking time: 15 minutes

Tomato & Butter Bean Soup

A rich tomato soup with creamy butterbeans to make it extra hearty. This one is wholesome, budget-friendly and perfect with a slice of bread for dipping.

INGREDIENTS:

1 onion, chopped

2 garlic cloves, crushed

400g (14oz) can chopped tomatoes

400g (14oz) can butter beans, rinsed and drained

500ml (18fl oz) vegetable stock

1 teaspoon Italian dried mixed herbs

STAPLE INGREDIENTS:

Pepper

Olive oil

Paprika

1　In a large pan over medium heat, sauté the onion and garlic in 1 tablespoon of oil for 3–4 minutes until softened.

2　Add the chopped tomatoes, butter beans, vegetable stock, herbs, ½ teaspoon of black pepper and ½ teaspoon of paprika, and simmer on a medium-high heat for 10 minutes.

3　Leave it chunky like a bean stew or blend it up for a smooth soup – both work and taste amazing!

4　Store in an airtight container in the refrigerator for up to 3 days or in the freezer for up to 3 months. Reheat on the stove or in the microwave, stirring halfway until steaming hot. If frozen, thaw overnight in the refrigerator for best results or reheat from frozen. You can add a little water if it is too thick.

Veggie Burrito Bowl

All the best bits of a burrito – rice, beans, salsa, guac – piled high in a bowl. It's colourful, hearty and completely veggie.

INGREDIENTS:

½ red pepper, cored, deseeded and diced

¼ red onion, diced

125g (4½oz) canned black beans or refried beans, drained

125g (4½oz) cooked rice

2 tablespoons guacamole or ½ avocado, diced

2 tablespoons salsa or 1 tomato, diced

STAPLE INGREDIENTS:

Salt

Pepper

Olive oil

Paprika

Cayenne pepper (optional)

1 Heat a little oil in a frying pan over a medium heat. Add the red pepper and red onion, and cook for 5–7 minutes until soft and starting to caramelize.

2 Add the beans to the pan, stir them in and cook for 2–3 minutes until warmed through. Season with salt, pepper, paprika and cayenne pepper for a little kick if desired.

3 Place the cooked rice in a bowl, spoon over the bean and pepper mixture, then top with the guacamole or diced avocado.

4 Finish with a generous spoonful of salsa or chopped tomato and serve straight away.

TIPS

Try this with my Classic Chunky Guacamole and Homemade Fresh Salsa on page 135 or add your favourite toppings, such as soured cream and chopped parsley or coriander.

Serves 1 · Prep time: 5 minutes · Cooking time: 7-12 minutes

Fancy Pizza Toast

A simple slice of toast transformed into the best pizza toast you'll ever eat.
It's is quick, fun and endlessly customizable.

INGREDIENTS:

1 slice of sourdough bread

½ burrata

2 large slices of tomato

2–3 tablespoons pizza sauce

½ tablespoon grated Parmesan cheese

½ teaspoon Italian dried mixed herbs
   or a few basil leaves

STAPLE INGREDIENTS:

Salt

Pepper

Olive oil

1   Preheat the grill to medium-high or preheat the air fryer to 200°C (400°F).

2   Brush both sides of the bread with olive oil and grill or air fry for 4–6 minutes, flipping halfway, until crisp and golden.

3   Tear the burrata and lay it on top of the toasted bread, then place the tomato slices on top and season with salt and pepper.

4   Return to the grill or air fryer for 2–4 minutes until the burrata starts to melt and the tomatoes soften slightly.

5   While the toast cooks, warm the pizza sauce gently in a pan or in the microwave in 30 second bursts until hot.

6   Spoon the hot pizza sauce over the toast, then sprinkle with Parmesan.

7   Place back under the grill or in the air fryer for 1–2 minutes more to melt the Parmesan.

8   Finish with a sprinkle of dried herbs or a few fresh basil leaves and serve straight away.

Sweet Chilli Chicken Wrap

Sweet and sticky chicken with just the right amount of heat, all wrapped up with crunchy greens. This wrap is quick to make and tastes amazing warm or cold.

INGREDIENTS:

1 chicken breast, cut into strips

¼ red pepper, cored, deseeded and thinly sliced

1 tablespoon mayonnaise

1 tablespoon sweet chilli sauce

Small handful of lettuce or spinach

1 large tortilla wrap

STAPLE INGREDIENTS:

Salt

Pepper

Olive oil

Paprika

Cayenne pepper (optional)

1 Place the chicken and pepper slices in a bowl, and season with salt, pepper, 1 teaspoon of paprika and a pinch of cayenne pepper if desired.

2 Cook the chicken and peppers in an air fryer at 180°C (350°F) for 10–12 minutes, or pan fry them over medium heat in a little oil, turning occasionally, for around 7–8 minutes until the chicken is cooked through and at least 75°C (167°F) when tested with a meat thermometer.

3 While the chicken and peppers cook, mix the mayo and sweet chilli sauce in a medium bowl.

4 Once cooked, transfer the chicken and peppers to the bowl and coat them in the sweet chilli mayo.

5 Place the lettuce or spinach in the centre of the tortilla wrap and spoon the mixture on top. Fold in the sides of the wrap, then roll the wrap tightly from the bottom up.

6 Place seam side down in a hot dry frying pan and toast for 1–2 minutes on each side. Slice it in half and serve.

Autumn Harvest Salad

This is packed with autumn flavours. It's crunchy, sweet, savoury; proof that salads don't have to be boring. For extra protein, add grilled chicken, crispy bacon, Parma ham or even hard-boiled eggs.

INGREDIENTS:

40g (1½oz) walnuts

100g (3½oz) mixed salad leaves

½ apple, thinly sliced or diced

30g (1oz) dried cranberries

50g (1¾oz) feta or other cheese, crumbled

Honey Mustard Vinaigrette (see below)

STAPLE INGREDIENTS:

Salt

Pepper

1 If you like extra crunch and flavour, lightly toast the walnuts in a dry frying pan over medium heat for 2–3 minutes until fragrant, then set aside to cool.

2 In a large bowl, toss together the mixed salad leaves, apple, cranberries and walnuts.

3 Crumble over the cheese and season with salt and pepper to taste.

4 Drizzle with the vinaigrette just before serving and toss gently to combine.

Honey Mustard Vinaigrette

Sweet, tangy and so delicious! This dressing goes with almost any salad and takes just minutes to make.

INGREDIENTS:

2 teaspoons balsamic vinegar

½ teaspoon yellow or Dijon mustard

2 teaspoons honey

STAPLE INGREDIENTS:

Salt

Olive oil

1 Place all the ingredients in a small bowl, ramekin or jar with 1 teaspoon of olive oil.

2 Add a pinch of salt and whisk (or shake if using a jar) until smooth and slightly thickened.

3 Taste and adjust to your liking – add a little more honey if you prefer it sweeter or more vinegar for extra tang.

4 Drizzle over your favourite salad and toss just before serving.

pictured overleaf

Pizza Salad

All the flavours of pizza, but in salad form. Add cooked chicken or pepperoni for extra protein.

INGREDIENTS:

1 pitta bread

4 tablespoons passata or pizza sauce

½ teaspoon Italian dried mixed herbs

1 Romaine lettuce, chopped

100g (3½oz) tomatoes, finely diced

70g (2½oz) mozzarella, torn

STAPLE INGREDIENTS:

Salt

Pepper

Olive oil

Paprika

1 Preheat your oven to 200°C, 180°C fan (400°F), Gas Mark 6 or air fryer to 180°C (350°F). Cut the pitta into little triangles and toss with a dash of olive oil, salt, pepper and a pinch of paprika. Spread them out on a baking tray or in the air fryer basket and bake for 6–10 minutes until golden and crisp.

2 In a small bowl, mix the passata with a drizzle of olive oil, the Italian herbs and a pinch of salt and pepper until smooth. Add a splash of water to loosen it if necessary. This is our 'pizza' dressing.

3 In a large bowl, combine the chopped lettuce, tomatoes and mozzarella.

4 Add the tomato dressing and toss until everything is evenly coated.

5 Top with the crispy pitta croûtons and enjoy!

Serves 1–2 · Prep time: 10 minutes

Creamy Avocado Salad

Inspired by the green goddess salad, this is quick to make and leaves you feeling properly satisfied.

INGREDIENTS:

1 avocado, halved

3 tablespoons Greek yogurt

Juice of ½ lemon

1 Baby Gem lettuce, chopped

½ cucumber, finely diced

2 spring onions, finely sliced

STAPLE INGREDIENTS:

Salt

Pepper

Olive oil (optional)

Cayenne pepper (optional)

1 Scoop the avocado flesh into a small bowl and mash with the Greek yogurt, lemon juice, salt and pepper to create a creamy dressing. If needed, add 1–2 tablespoons of water to loosen it to your desired consistency.

2 In a large bowl, combine the chopped lettuce, diced cucumber and sliced spring onions.

3 Add the avocado dressing and toss until everything is evenly coated.

4 Taste and adjust the seasoning. Add a drizzle of olive oil or even a pinch of cayenne pepper if you want a little kick. Serve straight away.

pictured overleaf

Serves 1 · Prep time: 10 minutes · Cooking time: 2–3 minutes (optional)

Crunchy Rainbow Wrap

Loaded with colourful veggies, this wrap looks just as good as it tastes –
a great way to brighten up lunchtime.

INGREDIENTS:

1 large tortilla wrap

2 tablespoons hummus

Handful of shredded red cabbage

¼ red pepper, cored, deseeded and
thinly sliced

½ avocado, sliced

½ burrata or other cheese

STAPLE INGREDIENTS:

Salt

Pepper

1   Place the wrap on a board and spread the hummus in a line across
the middle.

2   Layer the cabbage, red pepper and avocado over the hummus, then
tear the burrata over the top.

3   Season with salt and pepper, fold in the sides of the wrap, then roll
the wrap tightly from the bottom up.

4   Serve straight away, or place seam side down in a hot dry frying pan
and toast for 2–3 minutes on each side. Slice it in half and serve.

TIPS

Use a spinach or beetroot
wrap for extra colour.

For extra flavour, use a
flavoured hummus and
drizzle a little lemon juice
or tahini over the veggies.

Cheese & Ham Toastie Dippers

A cross between a classic ham and cheese toastie and French toast!
Serve with soup, ketchup or just on their own. They're ridiculously good.

INGREDIENTS:

4 slices of soft white bread

1 tablespoon butter, plus extra
   for frying

4 slices of cheese, such as Cheddar
   or Gouda

4 wafer-thin slices of ham

1 egg

2 tablespoons milk (any)

STAPLE INGREDIENTS:

Salt

Pepper

1 Lay the slices of bread on a board and remove the crusts if desired, then butter them.

2 On 2 of the slices, place a slice of cheese, then 2 slices of ham, followed by another slice of cheese. Top with the other slices of bread, butter sides down, to make 2 sandwiches.

3 Cut each sandwich into 3 equal rectangles.

4 In a medium bowl, whisk together the egg, milk and a pinch of salt and pepper.

5 Heat a little butter in a large nonstick frying pan over medium heat.

6 Dip each piece of sandwich into the egg mixture, coating all sides, then place straight into the pan.

7 Fry for 2–3 minutes on each side until golden and the cheese has melted. Serve straight away.

TIP

Serve these with
your favourite
dipping sauce.

Mexican-Style Chicken & Sweetcorn Soup

A warming soup full of flavour, with tender chicken, spices and a little kick of heat. It's cosy, comforting and a brilliant way to shake up your usual chicken soup.

INGREDIENTS:

1 red pepper, cored, deseeded and chopped

1 onion, chopped

400g (14oz) can chopped tomatoes

285g (10¼oz) can sweetcorn, drained

500ml (18fl oz) chicken stock

2 cooked chicken breasts, shredded

STAPLE INGREDIENTS:

Pepper

Olive oil

Smoked paprika

Cayenne pepper

1 In a large pan over medium heat, sauté the red pepper and onion in 1 tablespoon of oil for 3–4 minutes until softened.

2 Add the tomatoes, sweetcorn, chicken stock, ½ teaspoon of black pepper, ½ teaspoon of smoked paprika and a pinch of cayenne pepper. Simmer on a medium-high heat for 10 minutes.

3 Stir in the shredded chicken and heat through for 5 minutes or until you reach your desired thickness.

4 Store in an airtight container in the refrigerator for up to 3 days or in the freezer for up to 3 months. Reheat on the stove or in the microwave, stirring halfway until steaming hot. If frozen, thaw it overnight in the refrigerator for best results or reheat from frozen. You can add a little water if it is too thick.

TIP

Never reheat chicken soup then store it again. Always reheat fully only what you plan to eat.

Cheeseburger Bowl

Everything you love about a cheeseburger – juicy beef, cheese, onions and pickles – but served in a bowl without the bun. Fresh, filling, satisfying and a little bit lighter.

INGREDIENTS:

¼ onion, finely diced

200g (7oz) minced beef

2–3 slices of American cheese

2 big handfuls of shredded lettuce

1 small gherkin or pickle, sliced

2 tablespoons burger sauce or
   Everything Sauce (see below)

STAPLE INGREDIENTS:

Salt

Pepper

Olive oil

1 Heat a little oil in a frying pan over medium-low heat. Add the onion and a pinch of salt and cook for 8–10 minutes, stirring occasionally, until golden and caramelized. Transfer to a bowl and set aside.

2 Turn the heat up to medium-high. Add the minced beef to the pan, season with salt and pepper, and cook for 6–8 minutes, breaking it up with a spoon, until browned and fully cooked through.

3 Reduce the heat to low and lay the slices of cheese on top. Cover with a lid or plate and cook for 1–2 minutes until the cheese has melted.

4 Place the shredded lettuce in a serving bowl, then top with the cheesy beef, caramelized onion and sliced gherkin.

5 Finish with a generous drizzle of burger sauce and serve straight away.

Everything Sauce

This is creamy, tangy and good on pretty much everything. Perfect for burgers, wraps and fries.

INGREDIENTS:

3 tablespoons mayonnaise

2 tablespoons tomato ketchup

2 teaspoons yellow mustard

1 teaspoon Worcestershire sauce
   (optional)

STAPLE INGREDIENTS:

Salt (optional)

Paprika (optional)

1 In a small bowl, combine the mayonnaise, ketchup, mustard and Worcestershire sauce, if using.

2 Mix until smooth and creamy.

3 Taste and add ¼ teaspoon of paprika and salt if desired.

4 Chill for 10 minutes to let the flavours come together or use straight away.

Serves 1 · Prep time: 10 minutes · Cooking time: 5 minutes (optional)

Chicken Avocado Burrito

Juicy chicken, creamy avocado and plenty of flavour wrapped up in a soft tortilla.
This is fresh, filling and the perfect grab-and-go lunch.

INGREDIENTS:

1 large tortilla wrap

Handful of spinach

1 cooked chicken breast, chopped
   or shredded

½ avocado, sliced

70g (2½oz) cheese, such as mozzarella
   or burrata, chopped

2 tablespoons salsa or 1 tomato,
   chopped

STAPLE INGREDIENTS:

Salt

Pepper

1   Lay the wrap on a board. Arrange the spinach, chicken, avocado, cheese
    and salsa in a line across the middle to make rolling easier, then season
    with salt and pepper.

2   Fold in the sides of the wrap, then roll the wrap tightly from the
    bottom up to form a burrito.

3   Enjoy as it is or, for a toasted, warm finish, place seam side down in a hot
    dry frying pan and toast for 2–3 minutes on each side.

4   Slice in half and serve warm or cold.

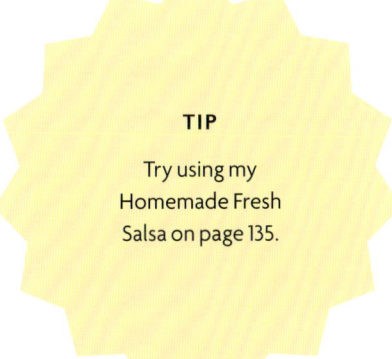

TIP

Try using my
Homemade Fresh
Salsa on page 135.

Pasta & Noodles

MARRY-ME CHICKEN PASTA **72**

ONE-PAN PESTO GNOCCHI **74**

HOISIN BEEF NOODLES **76**

TOMATO & BASIL SAUSAGE RIGATONI **78**

SUN-DRIED TOMATO PASTA **80**

ULTIMATE MAC 'N' CHEESE **82**

LEMON BUTTER PRAWN LINGUINE **84**

SUNDAY NIGHT SPAGHETTI & MEATBALLS **86**

COSY TUNA PASTA BAKE **88**

ONE-POT LASAGNE SOUP **90**

CHEESY HUNTER'S CHICKEN PASTA **92**

PEANUT BUTTER NOODLES **94**

CREAMY CAJUN CHICKEN PASTA **96**

GREEN GODDESS PASTA **98**

Marry-Me Chicken Pasta

I don't have the words for how good this pasta is — creamy, tomatoey, hearty and comforting, all the best things in one bowl. It's way quicker and easier to make than you'd expect.

INGREDIENTS:

2 chicken breasts

100g (3½oz) linguine

2 tablespoons tomato purée

70g (2½oz) sun-dried tomatoes in oil, drained and diced

200ml (7fl oz) single cream

85g (3oz) Parmesan cheese, grated

STAPLE INGREDIENTS:

Salt

Pepper

Olive oil

Paprika

Cayenne pepper

1 Place the chicken breasts between 2 sheets of baking paper and tenderize (flatten) them using a meat mallet or the base of a saucepan — this will help them cook more evenly and improve the texture.

2 Rub the chicken breasts all over with salt, pepper and 1 teaspoon of paprika to season.

3 Heat a large frying pan over a medium heat and spray with oil so the chicken doesn't stick, then cook the chicken for 5 minutes on each side, or until cooked through and at least 75°C (167°F) when tested with a meat thermometer.

4 Meanwhile, cook the linguine in a large pan of salted boiling water for 8–10 minutes, or according to the packet instructions.

5 When the chicken is cooked though, set it aside on a plate. Add the tomato purée and sun-dried tomatoes to the chicken pan, and cook on medium heat for about 1 minute.

6 Add 75ml (2½fl oz) of the pasta water and cook for a further 1–2 minutes, or until thickened.

7 Add the single cream, salt, pepper, ½ teaspoon of paprika, ½ teaspoon of cayenne pepper and the Parmesan and stir everything together until combined.

8 Drain the cooked linguine, then add it to the sauce and stir to coat.

9 Divide the pasta between 2 dishes and place the chicken, sliced, on top.

TIPS

For extra nutrients and flavour, add a handful of spinach in Step 7. Stir it into the sauce until it wilts.

Garnish with a few basil leaves before serving.

One-Pan Pesto Gnocchi

Soft, pillowy gnocchi cooked all in one pan with herby pesto.
Minimal washing up with maximum flavour.

INGREDIENTS:

325g (11½oz) gnocchi

150ml (5fl oz) single cream

40g (1½oz) pesto

Finely grated zest of 1 lemon,
    plus 1½ tablespoons juice

Small handful of chopped basil,
    plus extra to serve (optional)

STAPLE INGREDIENTS:

Salt

Pepper

Olive oil

1 Heat a drizzle of oil in a large frying pan over medium heat. Add the gnocchi and cook for 6–7 minutes, stirring occasionally, until golden and tender.

2 Add the cream, pesto, lemon zest, lemon juice, salt and pepper. Stir to combine and cook for 1–2 minutes until the sauce is hot and slightly thickened.

3 Stir through the chopped basil just before serving.

4 Divide between 2 bowls and top with extra basil if you like.

TIPS

For extra flavour, top with toasted pine nuts and Parmesan cheese.

For extra protein, fry two flattened chicken breasts for 5 minutes on each side, or until cooked through. Slice and serve on top of the gnocchi.

⩵ Hoisin Beef Noodles ⩵

Tender beef with a glossy hoisin sauce is tossed together with noodles
to create a dish big on flavour but surprisingly quick.

INGREDIENTS:

400g (14oz) fresh egg noodles or
200g (7oz) dried egg noodles
200g (7oz) thin-cut steak, such as
bavette, skirt or flank, thinly sliced
4 tablespoons soy sauce
125g (4¼oz) hoisin sauce
1 teaspoon garlic purée
1 spring onion, sliced

STAPLE INGREDIENTS:

Neutral oil, such as rapeseed

1 If using dried noodles, cook them according to the packet instructions, then rinse under cold water to prevent them from sticking together and set aside.

2 Heat a little oil in a large frying pan over medium-high heat. Add the beef strips and cook for 1–2 minutes per side, until browned. Avoid overcrowding the pan – cook in batches if necessary.

3 Add the soy sauce, hoisin sauce and garlic purée. Stir until combined to coat the beef in the sauce.

4 Add the noodles to the pan and toss everything together until well combined and heated through.

5 Stir through most of the spring onion, then divide the noodles between 2 bowls and sprinkle the remaining spring onion on top.

TIPS

Add some veggies, such as thinly sliced carrot or broccoli, in Step 2 for extra nutrients.

Top the finished dish with a sprinkle of chilli flakes and/or sesame seeds if you like.

Serves 2 · Prep time: 5 minutes · Cooking time: 10–15 minutes

Tomato & Basil Sausage Rigatoni

A hearty, classic combo of juicy sausages, fresh basil and rich tomato sauce. You'll appreciate a big bowl of this after a long day.

INGREDIENTS:

100g (3½oz) rigatoni

4 sausages, skinned

300g (10½oz) canned chopped tomatoes

2 tablespoons tomato purée

100ml (3½fl oz) single cream

Small handful of chopped basil, plus extra to serve (optional)

STAPLE INGREDIENTS:

Salt

Pepper

Olive oil

1 Cook the rigatoni in a large pan of salted boiling water for 8–10 minutes, or according to the packet instructions.

2 While the pasta is cooking, heat 1 tablespoon of oil in a large frying pan over a medium heat. Add the sausagemeat and cook for around 7 minutes, breaking it up, until fully cooked through and browned all over with no pink remaining.

3 Add the chopped tomatoes and tomato purée and cook for around 3 minutes until thickened slightly.

4 Pour in the cream and season with salt and pepper, then stir until combined. Add the basil.

5 Drain the pasta, then add it to the sauce and stir to coat it.

6 Divide between 2 bowls and top with a little more basil if desired.

Sun-Dried Tomato Pasta

A quick, no-fuss pasta packed with flavour thanks to the rich sun-dried tomatoes and Parmesan. It feels fancy, but it's one of the easiest dishes in the book.

INGREDIENTS:

125g (4¼oz) pasta, such as linguine or rigatoni

8 sun-dried tomatoes in oil, drained and diced

400g (14oz) can chopped tomatoes

200ml (7fl oz) single cream

30g (1oz) Parmesan cheese, grated, plus extra to serve (optional)

6 basil leaves, chopped, plus extra to serve (optional)

STAPLE INGREDIENTS:

Salt

Pepper

1 Cook the pasta in a large pan of salted boiling water for 8–10 minutes, or according to the packet instructions.

2 While the pasta is cooking, heat a large frying pan over a medium heat and cook the sun-dried tomatoes in about 1 tablespoon of oil from the jar for 1–2 minutes.

3 Pour in the chopped tomatoes and cook for 3–4 minutes until thickened slightly.

4 Pour in the cream, sprinkle over the Parmesan and season with salt and pepper. Stir until well combined, then add the basil and stir again.

5 Drain the pasta, then add it to the sauce and stir to coat it.

6 Divide between 2 bowls and add a little extra Parmesan and basil if desired.

Ultimate Mac 'n' Cheese

The ultimate cheesy hug in a bowl. Gooey, creamy and golden, this one never fails to make people happy. I love adding barbecue sauce to mine!

INGREDIENTS:

150g (5½oz) macaroni

30g (1oz) salted butter

30g (1oz) plain flour

400ml (14fl oz) whole milk

125g (4½oz) Cheddar cheese, grated

20g (¾oz) Parmesan cheese, grated,
    plus extra to serve (optional)

STAPLE INGREDIENTS:

Salt

Pepper

Paprika

1 Cook the macaroni in a large pan of salted boiling water for 8–10 minutes, or according to the packet instructions. Drain, transfer the pasta to a bowl and set aside.

2 In the same pan, melt the butter over medium heat. Stir in the flour and cook for 1 minute to form a paste (roux).

3 Slowly whisk in the milk, a little at a time, until smooth. Continue stirring for 4–5 minutes until the sauce thickens slightly.

4 Turn down the heat to low. Stir in the grated Cheddar and Parmesan until melted and smooth. Season with salt, pepper and a pinch of paprika to taste.

5 Add the cooked macaroni to the pan and stir to coat in the sauce. Heat through for 1–2 minutes.

6 Divide between 2 bowls and top with an extra sprinkle of Parmesan or paprika if you like.

TIP

For an extra cheesy, crispy topping, transfer the pasta and sauce to an ovenproof dish, top with a layer of grated Cheddar and Parmesan, then bake in the oven or air fryer until the cheese is golden.

Lemon Butter Prawn Linguine

Fresh, zesty and buttery all at once. The prawns soak up the lemony sauce beautifully, making this dish feel light but indulgent.

INGREDIENTS:

225g (8oz) raw prawns

100g (3½oz) linguine

35g (1¼oz) salted butter

Finely grated zest and juice of 1 lemon

40g (1½oz) Parmesan cheese, grated, plus extra to serve (optional)

2 tablespoons chopped parsley

STAPLE INGREDIENTS:

Salt

Pepper

Olive oil

Paprika

1 Tip the prawns into a medium bowl and season with salt, pepper and paprika, then set aside.

2 Cook the linguine in a large pan of salted boiling water for 8–10 minutes, or according to the packet instructions.

3 Meanwhile, heat a little oil in a large frying pan over medium-high heat. Add the prawns and cook for about 1 minute on each side until pink and just cooked through. Remove from the pan and set aside.

4 In the same pan, melt the butter, then stir in the lemon juice.

5 Drain the cooked linguine, reserving 125ml (4fl oz) of pasta water. Add the linguine to the pan, then add the prawns and parmesan. Pour in the reserved pasta water and stir everything together until the cheese melts and the sauce coats the pasta.

6 Stir through the chopped parsley and lemon zest. Divide between 2 bowls and top with extra Parmesan if you like.

Sunday Night Spaghetti & Meatballs

An all-time classic – juicy meatballs simmered in a rich tomato sauce, piled high on spaghetti. This is the ultimate crowd-pleaser.

INGREDIENTS:

325g (11½oz) meatballs

2 garlic cloves, chopped, or 2 teaspoons garlic purée

300g (10½oz) passata

200g (7oz) canned chopped tomatoes

100g (3½oz) spaghetti

6 basil leaves, chopped, plus extra to serve

STAPLE INGREDIENTS:

Salt

Pepper

Olive oil

1 Heat a drizzle of oil in a large frying pan over medium-high heat. Add the meatballs and cook for around 10 minutes, turning often, until browned on all sides. Remove from the pan and set aside.

2 In the same pan, sauté the fresh garlic over a low heat for about 2 minutes until fragrant.

3 Add the passata, chopped tomatoes, garlic purée (if not using fresh), ½ teaspoon of salt and ¼ teaspoon of pepper. Stir and simmer for 5 minutes until the sauce begins to thicken.

4 Meanwhile, cook the spaghetti in a large pan of salted boiling water for 8–10 minutes, or according to the packet instructions.

5 Return the meatballs to the pan with the sauce. Simmer for a further 10 minutes until the meatballs are cooked through and the sauce is thickened to your liking. Stir through the chopped basil.

6 Drain the spaghetti, divide it between 2 bowls, spoon over the meatballs and sauce and top with extra basil.

TIP

Feel free to sprinkle a little Parmesan on top for extra flavour.

Cosy Tuna Pasta Bake

A proper family favourite – tomatoey and cheesy, with a golden topping.
This is comfort food you'll keep coming back to.

INGREDIENTS:

125g (4¼oz) fusilli
400g (14oz) can chopped tomatoes
2 tablespoons tomato purée
1 teaspoon dried mixed herbs
145g (5¼oz) can tuna, drained
100g (3½oz) grated mozzarella cheese

STAPLE INGREDIENTS:

Salt
Pepper
Olive oil
Paprika

1 Preheat your oven to 200°C, 180°C fan (400°F), Gas Mark 6.

2 Cook the fusilli in a large pan of salted boiling water for 7–8 minutes, or 1–2 minutes less than the packet instructions.

3 Meanwhile, heat a drizzle of oil in a large frying pan over medium heat. Add the chopped tomatoes, tomato purée, mixed herbs, salt, pepper and a pinch of paprika. Stir well and simmer for 5–7 minutes until slightly thickened.

4 Drain the pasta, then stir the tuna and the pasta into the sauce until well combined.

5 Pour the mixture into an ovenproof dish, spread it out evenly, then top with the grated mozzarella.

6 Bake in the oven for 15–20 minutes until the cheese is golden. Divide between 2 bowls and serve hot.

⫶ One-Pot Lasagne Soup ⫶

Everything you love about lasagne, but in a cosy bowl with less effort.
It's hearty, cheesy and way easier than layering pasta sheets.

INGREDIENTS:

250g (9oz) minced beef

3 tablespoons tomato purée

400g (14oz) can chopped tomatoes

400ml (14fl oz) beef stock

100g (3½oz) lasagne sheets, broken
   into pieces

100ml (3½fl oz) double cream or 100g
   (3½oz) mozzarella cheese, chopped

STAPLE INGREDIENTS:

Salt

Pepper

Olive oil

1 Heat a little oil in a large saucepan over medium heat. Add the minced beef, season with salt and pepper, and cook for 5 minutes until browned, breaking it up as it cooks.

2 Stir in the tomato purée and cook for 1–2 minutes, then add the chopped tomatoes and beef stock, and season with pepper.

3 Bring to a simmer, then add the broken lasagne sheets. Cook over medium heat for 10–12 minutes, stirring occasionally, until the pasta is tender and the soup has thickened slightly.

4 Turn the heat to low, then stir in the cream or the mozzarella until melted. Divide between 2 bowls and serve while still hot.

TIPS

Add 1 teaspoon of Italian dried mixed herbs in Step 2 if you like.

You could also sprinkle over some grated Cheddar or Parmesan after serving to make it extra cheesy.

Cheesy Hunter's Chicken Pasta

Think barbecue chicken, melted cheese and pasta all in one dish.
Smoky, saucy and seriously satisfying.

INGREDIENTS:

100g (3½oz) rigatoni

2 chicken breasts

3 teaspoons barbecue seasoning

200g (7oz) canned chopped tomatoes

4 tablespoons barbecue sauce

60g (2¼oz) mozzarella cheese,
    chopped

STAPLE INGREDIENTS:

Salt

Olive oil

1 Cook the rigatoni in a large pan of salted boiling water for 8–10 minutes, or according to the packet instructions.

2 While the pasta is cooking, place the chicken breasts between 2 sheets of baking paper and tenderize (flatten) them using a meat mallet or the base of a saucepan – this will help them cook more evenly and improve the texture.

3 Rub the chicken breasts all over with 2 teaspoons of the barbecue seasoning.

4 Heat a large frying pan over a medium heat and spray with oil so the chicken doesn't stick, then cook the chicken for 5 minutes on each side, or until cooked through and at least 75°C (167°F) when tested with a meat thermometer. Remove from the pan and slice into strips.

5 In the same pan, add the chopped tomatoes, remaining barbecue seasoning and the barbecue sauce. Stir to combine and let it bubble for 3–4 minutes until slightly thickened.

6 Drain the pasta, then add it to the sauce and stir until evenly coated. Add the sliced chicken on top, then sprinkle over the mozzarella. Place a lid on the pan and let it sit for 1–2 minutes until the cheese has melted.

7 Divide into 2 bowls and serve while still hot. Enjoy!

TIP

Drizzle the finished dish with extra barbecue sauce and add a sprinkle of chopped parsley, if you like.

Serves 2 · Prep time: 5 minutes · Cooking time: 8–14 minutes

Peanut Butter Noodles

Creamy, nutty and a little bit addictive, these quick noodles are
proof that peanut butter belongs in savoury dishes too.

INGREDIENTS:

400g (14oz) fresh egg noodles
    or 200g (7oz) dried egg noodles
1 carrot, finely sliced
2 garlic cloves, crushed, or 2 teaspoons
    garlic purée
4 tablespoons smooth peanut butter
4 tablespoons light or dark soy sauce
2 tablespoons honey or maple syrup

STAPLE INGREDIENTS:

Neutral oil, such as rapeseed

1 If using dried noodles, cook them according to the packet instructions, then rinse under cold water to prevent them from sticking together and set aside.

2 Heat a little oil in a large frying pan over medium heat, then add the sliced carrot and garlic, and cook for 1–2 minutes until the carrot has slightly softened.

3 Add the peanut butter, soy sauce, honey or maple syrup and 6 tablespoons of water to loosen the sauce. Stir everything together.

4 Once smooth, add the noodles and toss them in the sauce to warm them through for 5–6 minutes. Add more water to loosen the sauce if needed.

5 Divide between 2 bowls and serve warm.

TIP

This basic recipe is very flexible – add extra veggies and toppings, such as cooked broccoli, chopped spring onion, sesame seeds or chilli flakes.

Serves 2 · Prep time: 5 minutes · Cooking time: 15 minutes

Creamy Cajun Chicken Pasta

Creamy and spicy, with just the right amount of kick, this pasta is pure comfort food with a little extra attitude.

INGREDIENTS:

2 chicken breasts

5 teaspoons Cajun seasoning

1 large red pepper, cored, deseeded and cut into thin strips

100g (3½oz) rigatoni

250ml (9fl oz) double cream

30g (1oz) Parmesan cheese, grated, plus extra to serve

STAPLE INGREDIENTS:

Olive oil

1 Place the chicken breasts between 2 sheets of baking paper and tenderize (flatten) them using a meat mallet or the base of a saucepan – this will help them cook more evenly and improve the texture.

2 Rub the chicken breasts all over with 2 teaspoons of the Cajun seasoning.

3 Heat a large frying pan over a medium heat and spray with oil so the chicken doesn't stick, then cook the chicken for 5 minutes on each side, or until cooked through and at least 75°C (167°F) when tested with a meat thermometer, adding the red pepper to the pan when you flip the chicken.

4 Meanwhile, cook the rigatoni in a large pan of salted boiling water for 8–10 minutes, or according to the packet instructions.

5 When the chicken is cooked through, set it aside on a plate. Add the double cream, remaining Cajun seasoning and the Parmesan to the peppers in the pan and stir well until combined.

6 Drain the pasta and add it to the sauce, then stir to coat.

7 Divide between 2 bowls and place the chicken on top. Serve with some extra Parmesan alongside.

TIP

Sprinkle with chopped parsley for extra flavour and colour.

Serves 2 · Prep time: 5 minutes · Cooking time: 8–10 minutes

Green Goddess Pasta

This fresh, vibrant and creamy green sauce makes a wholesome and comforting pasta dish that just happens to be packed with veggies.

INGREDIENTS:

150g (5½oz) rigatoni or fusilli

1 large ripe avocado, halved

Large handful of basil leaves,
     plus extra to serve

30g (1oz) baby spinach

40g (1½oz) Parmesan cheese, grated,
     plus extra to serve

2 tablespoons Greek or plain yogurt

STAPLE INGREDIENTS:

Salt

Pepper

Olive oil

1 Cook the pasta in a large pan of salted boiling water for 8–10 minutes, or according to the packet instructions. Drain, reserving the pasta water.

2 Scoop the avocado flesh into a blender with the basil, spinach, Parmesan, yogurt, 2 teaspoons of oil and 4 tablespoons of the reserved pasta water. Season generously with salt and pepper, then blend until smooth.

3 Pour the green sauce over the cooked pasta and stir it through to coat evenly. Add a splash of warm water if needed to loosen the sauce.

4 Divide between 2 bowls and top with an extra sprinkle of Parmesan and some more basil leaves.

Dinner

STICKY TERIYAKI CHICKEN RICE BOWL 102

GARLIC PARMESAN CHICKEN TENDERS 104

HOT HONEY HALLOUMI RICE BOWL 106

CHEESEBURGER TACOS 108

CRISPY CHICKEN TACOS 109

SOY-GLAZED SALMON RICE BOWL 112

BANG BANG CHICKEN SKEWERS 114

DOUBLE SMASH CHEESEBURGER 116

CRISPY CHICKPEA SWEET POTATOES 118

LOADED CHILLI CHEESE FRIES 120

BBQ PULLED PORK SANDWICH 122

Sticky Teriyaki Chicken Rice Bowl

This rice bowl is the kind of dinner you'll want on repeat. The sweet, sticky chicken is served with broccoli over a bowl of steamed rice.

INGREDIENTS:

100g (3½oz) jasmine or basmati rice

2 chicken breasts

150g (5½oz) broccoli florets

4 tablespoons teriyaki sauce

1 tablespoon honey

1 spring onion, chopped

STAPLE INGREDIENTS:

Salt

Pepper

Neutral oil, such as rapeseed

1 Bring 200ml (7fl oz) of water to the boil in a saucepan with a pinch of salt. Rinse the rice under cold water, then add it to the pan. Bring back to the boil, cover the pan, then reduce to a simmer and cook for 10–12 minutes until fluffy. Turn off the heat and set aside with the lid on for 5 minutes.

2 While the rice is cooking, place the chicken breasts between 2 sheets of baking paper and tenderize (flatten) them using a meat mallet or the base of a saucepan – this will help them cook more evenly and improve the texture. Season on both sides with salt and pepper.

3 Heat a large frying pan over medium heat and spray with oil so the chicken doesn't stick, then cook the chicken for 5 minutes on each side, or until cooked through and at least 75°C (167°F) when tested with a meat thermometer. Slice into strips and set aside.

4 While the chicken is cooking, cook the broccoli to your liking. Steam it over a pan of boiling water for 5–6 minutes or microwave it with a splash of water for 3–4 minutes. It should be tender but not mushy.

5 Set the frying pan back over low heat, then add the teriyaki sauce and honey. Stir together for about 1 minute until combined and warmed through, then return the chicken to the pan and coat it in the sauce.

6 Serve the chicken over the rice with the broccoli on the side. Top with the spring onion to add colour and flavour.

TIPS

You could use 250g (9oz) of ready-cooked rice if you prefer; simply heat according to the packet instructions.

Serve with a sprinkling of toasted sesame seeds if you have some.

Serves 2 · Prep time: 10 minutes · Cooking time: 10–20 minutes

Garlic Parmesan Chicken Tenders

Crispy, garlicky and loaded with Parmesan, these are so moreish you'll be fighting over the last piece. Perfect for dunking into your favourite sauce or piled into wraps or sandwiches.

INGREDIENTS:

60g (2¼oz) cornflakes

300g (10½oz) chicken breast mini fillets

1 large egg, beaten

40g (1½oz) salted butter

1 teaspoon garlic purée

2 tablespoons grated Parmesan cheese

STAPLE INGREDIENTS:

Salt

Pepper

Paprika

1 If cooking the chicken in an oven, preheat to 220°C, 200°C fan (425°F), Gas Mark 7 and line a baking tray with foil.

2 Put the cornflakes into a food processor and process until roughly crushed. Alternatively, put them into a plastic bag and crush with a rolling pin, then pour into a bowl.

3 Season the chicken with salt, pepper and paprika. Coat the chicken in the egg, letting any excess drip off, then in the crushed cornflakes, making sure you pat them really firmly on both sides of the chicken.

4 Transfer the coated chicken breast mini fillets to your foil-lined tray if baking in the oven, or to your air fryer basket, making sure they're not touching each other. Air fry at 180°C (350°F) for 10–12 minutes, or cook in the oven for 18–20 minutes, until the chicken is cooked through and at least 75°C (167°F) when tested with a meat thermometer.

5 While the chicken is cooking, melt the butter in a small pan or in the microwave, then stir in the garlic purée. Dip the chicken pieces in the butter, letting any excess drip off. Transfer them to a plate and sprinkle over the Parmesan.

TIP

Add a sprinkle of finely chopped fresh coriander to the garlic butter if you wish.

Serves 2 · Prep time: 10 minutes · Cooking time: 20–30 minutes

Hot Honey Halloumi Rice Bowl

Crispy, golden halloumi coated in sweet and spicy hot honey. It's the perfect balance of flavours. Served with rice and veggies, this is a quick dinner that tastes like something special.

INGREDIENTS:

125g (4½oz) jasmine or basmati rice

2 tablespoons hot honey

2 tablespoons light or dark soy sauce

1 red pepper, cored, deseeded and finely sliced

200g (7oz) green beans and/or sugar snap peas

200g (7oz) halloumi, sliced

STAPLE INGREDIENTS:

Salt

Pepper

Neutral oil, such as rapeseed

1 Rinse the rice and cook it in a large pan of salted boiling water for 10–12 minutes, or according to the packet instructions.

2 In a small bowl, mix the hot honey with the soy sauce until combined.

3 Heat a little oil in a frying pan over medium heat. Add the red pepper and green beans and/or sugar snap peas, and season with salt and pepper. Sauté for 8–10 minutes until soft and lightly charred, then remove from the pan and set aside.

4 In the same pan, fry the halloumi slices for 2–3 minutes on each side until crisp and golden.

5 In the final minute, drizzle the hot honey mixture over the halloumi in the pan. Let it bubble and coat the cheese.

6 Drain the rice and divide between 2 bowls. Top with the veggies and hot honey-glazed halloumi. Spoon over any extra glaze from the pan and serve straight away.

TIPS

If you can't find hot honey, mix 1–2 teaspoons of hot sauce into regular honey, depending on your spice tolerance.

You can sprinkle with a few chilli flakes before serving if you like extra spice.

Cheeseburger Tacos

If a burger and a taco had a baby, this would be it! These went viral online for all the right reasons. Think juicy, crispy beef, warm toasted tortillas and all your favourite toppings.

INGREDIENTS:

250g (9oz) minced beef or
    burger patties
4 mini tortilla wraps
4 slices of American cheese
Handful of shredded lettuce
2 tomatoes, chopped
Burger sauce or Everything Sauce
    (see page 66)

STAPLE INGREDIENTS:

Salt
Pepper
Olive oil

1 Split the minced beef or burger patties into 4 equal portions and roll them into balls.

2 Spread the meat evenly over one side of each tortilla, all the way to the edges, then season with salt and pepper.

3 Heat a large frying pan over medium-high heat and spray with a little oil. Place the tortillas, meat side down, in the pan and cook for 2–3 minutes or until browned and cooked through. The meat will shrink a fair bit.

4 Flip each tortilla over, then place a slice of cheese on top of the meat and cover the pan with a lid for 30–60 seconds to melt the cheese and lightly toast the tortilla. (You may need to cook the tortillas in batches, depending on the size of your frying pan.)

5 Remove the tortillas from the pan, then top with shredded lettuce, chopped tomatoes and burger sauce.

TIPS

Feel free to swap out or add extra toppings, such as sliced gherkins.

Enjoy these tacos as they are, or serve with a side salad for a larger meal.

pictured overleaf

Crispy Chicken Tacos

Juicy, cheesy chicken, wrapped in crispy golden tortillas. They're super quick and easy, and perfect for dipping in your favourite sauce.

INGREDIENTS:

2 chicken breasts

½ red pepper, cored, deseeded and finely diced

1 small onion, diced

1 tablespoon tomato purée

6 mini tortilla wraps

100g (3½oz) Cheddar or mozzarella cheese, grated

STAPLE INGREDIENTS:

Salt

Pepper

Olive oil

Paprika

Cayenne pepper

1 Dice the chicken into tiny pieces, then place in a bowl with a drizzle of oil and season with salt, pepper, paprika and a pinch of cayenne pepper for a little heat. Coat well.

2 Heat a little oil in a large frying pan over medium heat. Add the chicken, diced pepper and onion, and cook for 6–8 minutes, stirring, until the chicken is cooked through (at least 75°C/167°F when tested with a meat thermometer) and lightly golden.

3 Add the tomato purée and 1 tablespoon of water to the pan and stir through for 1–2 minutes to coat the chicken and veggies. Transfer to a plate and carefully wipe the pan clean.

4 Place as many mini tortillas as will comfortably fit in the pan and sprinkle cheese over one side of each. Top the cheese with a spoonful of the chicken and veggie mix.

5 Fold the tortillas in half and press down gently. Cook for 2–3 minutes on each side over medium heat until golden and crisp, and the cheese has melted. Repeat with the remaining tortillas and filling.

TIP

Serve these tacos with your favourite sauces or dips, such as soured cream and Classic Chunky Guacamole (see page 135).

pictured overleaf

Serves 2 · Prep time: 10 minutes · Cooking time: 15 minutes

Soy-Glazed Salmon Rice Bowl

This salmon is glazed in a sticky soy sauce and served over rice with fresh veggies. It's light, fresh and full of flavour, the perfect midweek meal.

INGREDIENTS:

125g (4½oz) jasmine or basmati rice

4 tablespoons light or dark soy sauce

2 tablespoons honey

2 salmon fillets

200g (7oz) tenderstem broccoli

1 spring onion, chopped

STAPLE INGREDIENTS:

Neutral oil, such as rapeseed

1 Rinse the rice and cook it in a large pan of salted boiling water for 10–12 minutes, or according to the packet instructions.

2 In a small bowl, mix the soy sauce with the honey to make a simple glaze.

3 Pat the salmon fillets dry with kitchen paper, then cut them into bite-sized cubes, removing the skin first if you prefer.

4 While the rice is cooking, heat a little oil in a nonstick frying pan over a medium heat, then cook the salmon bites for 3–4 minutes, turning frequently.

5 Pour the soy glaze over the salmon and cook for another 2–3 minutes, turning the salmon bites to coat them in the sauce. Make sure the salmon is cooked through.

6 Meanwhile, cook the broccoli to your liking. Steam it over a pan of boiling water for 5–6 minutes or microwave it with a splash of water for 3–4 minutes. It should be tender but not mushy.

7 Drain the rice and divide between 2 bowls. Place the salmon bites and broccoli on top and spoon over any remaining glaze from the pan. Sprinkle with chopped spring onion and enjoy!

TIPS

Feel free to use microwavable rice for speed and ease.

Sprinkle over some sesame seeds for extra texture and flavour, or add chilli flakes to the sauce for a little kick.

Bang Bang Chicken Skewers

These juicy chicken skewers are coated with a creamy, spicy-sweet bang bang sauce that makes every bite pop. Perfect for a quick dinner, they're also great if you're cooking for friends.

INGREDIENTS:

2 chicken breasts

4 tablespoons mayonnaise

2 tablespoons sweet chilli sauce

1 tablespoon sriracha

1 teaspoon honey

Handful of chopped parsley

STAPLE INGREDIENTS:

Salt

Pepper

Neutral oil, such as rapeseed

Paprika

Cayenne pepper

1 Soak 4 wooden skewers in water for 20 minutes to prevent them from burning.

2 If cooking the chicken in an oven, preheat to 220°C, 200°C fan (425°F), Gas Mark 7 and line a baking tray with foil.

3 Cut the chicken into bite-sized cubes and place in a medium bowl.

4 Add a drizzle of oil, then season with 1–2 teaspoons of paprika, ½ teaspoon of cayenne pepper, salt and pepper, and toss to coat evenly. Push the chicken pieces onto the soaked skewers.

5 Transfer the skewers to your foil-lined tray if baking in the oven, or to your air fryer basket, making sure they're not touching each other. Air fry at 180°C (350°F) for 10 minutes, or cook in the oven for 18–20 minutes, until the chicken is cooked through and at least 75°C (167°F) when tested with a meat thermometer.

6 While the chicken is cooking, mix the mayonnaise, sweet chilli sauce, sriracha and honey together in a small bowl until smooth.

7 Once the chicken is cooked, brush the sauce all over to coat, then sprinkle with chopped parsley.

TIP

Serve the skewers with coconut rice or noodles and steamed veggies, or in a wrap or pitta with salad.

Double Smash Cheeseburger

Smash burgers are all about those crispy, golden edges and gooey melted cheese. This is hands down one of the best burgers you'll make at home.

INGREDIENTS:

300g (10½oz) minced beef

½ onion, sliced

4 slices of American cheese

2 burger buns

4 tablespoons burger sauce or Everything Sauce (see page 66)

STAPLE INGREDIENTS:

Salt

Pepper

Olive oil

1 Divide the minced beef into 4 equal loose balls and season generously with salt and pepper.

2 Heat a large frying pan over high heat with a little bit of oil. Place the mince balls in the pan, then place the onion slices on top and smash them flat with the back of a sturdy spatula, pressing down until they're very thin. (You may need to cook them in batches.)

3 Cook for 2–3 minutes until crispy underneath. Flip them over, then place a slice of cheese on top of each patty and cook for 1–2 minutes until the burgers are cooked to your liking. If you have a lid for your pan, place this on top to help the cheese melt.

4 Split the buns and lightly toast the cut sides in a dry frying pan.

5 Spread the sauce on the bun halves, then layer 2 burger patties on each base and replace the tops. Serve immediately with your favourite sides.

TIPS

I suggest using minced beef with about 20 per cent fat.

Add your own extras, such as pickles, lettuce and tomato (my fave), or swap out the sauce for a simple ketchup or mayo.

Serves 2 · Prep time: 5 minutes · Cooking time: 50–55 minutes

Crispy Chickpea Sweet Potatoes

You won't feel you're missing out with this simple, filling and meat-free dish. The spiced crunchy chickpeas and crispy kale make it hearty and satisfying.

INGREDIENTS:

2 sweet potatoes

400g (14oz) can chickpeas, rinsed and drained

100g (3½oz) kale, stems removed, roughly chopped

2 tablespoons tahini

2 tablespoons honey

1 garlic clove, crushed, or 1 teaspoon garlic purée

STAPLE INGREDIENTS:

Salt

Pepper

Olive oil

Paprika

Cayenne pepper (optional)

1 Preheat your oven to 200°C, 180°C fan (400°F), Gas Mark 6 and line 2 baking trays with baking paper. Prick the sweet potatoes a few times with a fork, place in an ovenproof dish and roast for 50–55 minutes until soft on the inside and crispy on the outside.

2 While the sweet potatoes are cooking, pat the chickpeas dry with kitchen paper and place in a medium bowl. Toss them in a little oil, paprika, salt, pepper and a pinch of cayenne pepper for a little heat if you like. Spread them out on a lined baking tray and roast for 25–30 minutes, shaking them halfway, until crisp and golden.

3 With 10 minutes to go, toss the kale in a little oil, salt and pepper, spread out on the other lined baking tray and roast for 8–10 minutes until crisp at the edges.

4 In a small bowl, mix the tahini, honey, garlic and a pinch of salt with 1 tablespoon of water to loosen into a drizzling sauce.

5 Once everything is cooked, slice the sweet potatoes open and gently mash the insides with a fork.

6 Top the sweet potatoes with the crispy kale, roasted chickpeas and a drizzle of the tahini sauce, and serve straight away.

Loaded Chilli Cheese Fries

Crispy fries smothered in veggie chilli, melty cheese and all the toppings. This is proper comfort food, the kind you'll want to dive into with a fork (but don't be surprised if you end up using your fingers).

INGREDIENTS:

500g (1lb 2oz) potatoes

1 red onion, diced

400g (14oz) can mixed beans or kidney beans, rinsed and drained

1 tablespoon tomato purée

225g (8oz) canned chopped tomatoes

40g (1½oz) Cheddar cheese, grated

STAPLE INGREDIENTS:

Salt

Pepper

Olive oil

Paprika

Cayenne pepper

1 Preheat your oven to 200°C, 180°C fan (400°F), Gas Mark 6. Cut the potatoes into fries about 1cm (½ inch) thick, then toss them in oil, salt, pepper and paprika. Spread them out on a baking tray and cook for 30–35 minutes until tender and crisp. The thicker your fries, the longer they'll take to cook.

2 While the fries are cooking, heat a little oil in a large pan over medium heat and cook the red onion for 5–6 minutes until soft.

3 Add the beans, tomato purée, chopped tomatoes, a pinch of salt, ½ teaspoon of paprika and a pinch of cayenne pepper. Simmer for 8–10 minutes until thickened.

4 Once the fries are cooked, transfer them to an ovenproof dish and spoon the bean chilli over the top.

5 Sprinkle over the grated cheese and return to the oven for about 5 minutes until melted. Serve hot.

TIPS

I like Maris Piper potatoes, but feel free to swap them for sweet potatoes or frozen fries.

Don't forget to add your favourite toppings, such as soured cream, fresh coriander or parsley and guacamole.

Serves 4 · Prep time: 10 minutes · Cooking time: 3–8 hours

BBQ Pulled Pork Sandwich

Tender pork is slow-cooked to perfection in smoky barbecue sauce, then piled high in soft buns. It's juicy and saucy, and you'll definitely need extra napkins.

INGREDIENTS:

1.5kg (3lb 5oz) boneless, skinless pork shoulder
250g (9oz) barbecue sauce, plus extra to serve
2 tablespoons tomato purée
2 tablespoons honey
4 brioche buns
Coleslaw (optional)

STAPLE INGREDIENTS:

Salt
Pepper
Olive oil
Paprika

1 Cut the pork shoulder into large chunks and season all over with salt, pepper and paprika.

2 Heat a little oil in a frying pan over medium-high heat and sear the pork for 2–3 minutes on each side until browned. This is optional, but adds extra flavour.

3 In a small bowl, mix together the barbecue sauce, tomato purée and honey.

4 Slow cooker method (preferred): Place the seared pork in the slow cooker and pour over the sauce. Place the lid on and cook on low for 8 hours or high for 5–6 hours, until the pork is tender and falling apart.

Oven method: Preheat the oven to 160°C, 140°C fan (325°F), Gas Mark 3. Place the pork in a deep ovenproof dish and pour over the sauce. Cover tightly with foil and bake for 3–3½ hours, until tender and falling apart.

5 Once cooked, shred the pork using 2 forks and stir through the sauce until well coated.

6 Split the buns and lightly toast the cut sides in a dry frying pan. Divide the pork into 4 portions and pile it into the buns. Try not to add too much of the juice or the buns will become soggy.

7 Add some extra barbecue sauce and a helping of coleslaw if you like.

8 To reheat any leftover meat, preheat the oven to 120°C, 100°C fan (250°F), Gas Mark ½. Arrange the pulled pork in a single layer in an ovenproof dish and add a drizzle of barbecue sauce to help retain moisture. Cover the dish with foil to trap steam and cook for 30 minutes or until it reaches at least 74°C (165°F) when tested with a meat thermometer.

TIP

I love adding a slice of grilled pineapple to my pulled pork sandwiches. You can use fresh or tinned – just place it in a pan or under the grill for a few minutes on each side.

Snacks & Sides

HOMEMADE BAKED BEANS 126

GOLDEN ROASTED VEGETABLES 128

CHEESY MASHED POTATO 130

CHEESY BROCCOLI BAKE 132

EASY AIR FRYER TORTILLA CHIPS 134

CLASSIC CHUNKY GUACAMOLE / HOMEMADE FRESH SALSA 135

MINI CARAMELIZED ONION SAUSAGE ROLLS 138

STICKY GLAZED MEATBALLS 140

FRESH TOMATO BAGUETTE 142

GARLIC BREAD & PIZZA BAGUETTE 144

Homemade Baked Beans

Rich, smoky and so much tastier than the tinned version, these beans
are perfect on toast or alongside a cooked breakfast.

INGREDIENTS:

1 tablespoon tomato purée

300g (10½oz) passata

1 tablespoon brown sugar, honey
    or maple syrup

400g (14oz) can cannellini or haricot
    beans, rinsed and drained

STAPLE INGREDIENTS:

Salt

Pepper

Olive oil

Paprika

1   Heat 1 tablespoon of olive oil in a saucepan over medium heat. Stir in
    the tomato purée and 1 teaspoon of paprika and cook for 1–2 minutes
    to release flavour.

2   Add the passata, sugar, salt and pepper. Stir well, then bring to a simmer.

3   Tip in the beans and stir to coat. Simmer gently for 12–15 minutes,
    stirring occasionally, until the sauce thickens and clings to the beans.

4   Taste and adjust the seasoning if necessary.

TIP

Serve hot on toast
with eggs if you like.

Serves 2 · Prep time: 5 minutes · Cooking time: 20–25 minutes

Golden Roasted Vegetables

Caramelized with crispy edges, these simple and colourful veggies are a great way to pack in flavour and go with just about any meal. Vegetables that actually taste good!

INGREDIENTS:

1 red pepper, cored, deseeded and
   cut into strips
1 large carrot, cut into batons
200g (7oz) broccoli florets
200g (7oz) cauliflower florets
Juice of ½ lemon (optional)

STAPLE INGREDIENTS:

Salt
Pepper
Olive oil
Paprika

1 Preheat your oven to 200°C, 180°C fan (400°F), Gas Mark 6.

2 Spread all the vegetables out on a large baking tray. Drizzle with 2 tablespoons of olive oil, season with salt, pepper and a pinch of paprika, then toss to coat evenly.

3 Roast for 20–25 minutes, stirring once, until the edges of the veggies are golden and caramelized.

4 Remove from the oven and squeeze over the lemon juice if you like. Toss the veg well. Serve immediately.

TIP

Serve these roasted veg as a side with chicken, beef, fish or a veggie main.

⇒ Cheesy Mashed Potato ⇐

Fluffy, creamy, cheesy and totally irresistible, this is the
perfect side to accompany almost anything.

INGREDIENTS:

500g (1lb 2oz) floury potatoes,
    such as Maris Piper
40g (1½oz) butter
80ml (3fl oz) whole milk
80g (2¾oz) Cheddar cheese, grated
20g (¾oz) Parmesan cheese, grated

STAPLE INGREDIENTS:

Salt
Pepper

1　Peel and chop the potatoes into 3–4cm (1¼–1½ inch) chunks. Place them in a saucepan of salted water and bring to the boil. Simmer for 15–20 minutes until tender when pierced with a knife.

2　Drain well, then return the potatoes to the pan (off the heat) and allow them to sit for 1–2 minutes to steam dry. Don't skip this step, otherwise the mash can end up a bit watery.

3　Mash the potatoes until smooth. Add the butter and milk, then beat with a wooden spoon until creamy.

4　Stir in the Cheddar and Parmesan until melted and combined, then season generously with salt and pepper to taste.

TIP

Serve hot as a side dish with your favourite meal, such as the Garlic Parmesan Chicken Tenders on page 105.

Serves 2 · Prep time: 5 minutes · Cooking time: 20–25 minutes

Cheesy Broccoli Bake

Tender broccoli smothered in a creamy cheese sauce and baked until golden – this is comfort food disguised as a veggie side.

INGREDIENTS:

1 teaspoon butter

1 tablespoon plain flour

200ml (7fl oz) whole milk

80g (2¾oz) Cheddar cheese, grated

20g (¾oz) Parmesan cheese, grated

300g (10½oz) broccoli florets

STAPLE INGREDIENTS:

Salt

Pepper

1   Preheat your oven to 190°C, 170°C fan (375°F), Gas Mark 5.

2   In a small saucepan, melt the butter over medium heat. Stir in the flour and cook for 1 minute to form a paste (roux).

3   Slowly whisk in the milk, a little at a time, until smooth. Continue stirring for 4–5 minutes until the sauce thickens slightly.

4   Turn down the heat to low. Stir in three-quarters of the grated Cheddar and all the Parmesan until melted and smooth. Season with salt and pepper.

5   Meanwhile, steam the broccoli for 4–5 minutes over a pan of boiling water or splash with a little water and cook in the microwave until just tender, then drain well.

6   Place the broccoli in an ovenproof dish, pour over the cheese sauce and sprinkle the remaining Cheddar on top. Bake for 12–15 minutes until golden and bubbling.

Easy Air Fryer Tortilla Chips

These crispy tortilla chips are made in an air fryer with just a drizzle of oil and seasonings. They're quick, crunchy and the perfect partner for salsa or guac.

INGREDIENTS:

2 large corn or wheat tortilla wraps, cut into triangles

STAPLE INGREDIENTS:

Salt

Pepper

Olive oil

Paprika

1 Preheat your air fryer to 160°C (325°F). Alternatively, preheat your oven to 180°C, 160°C fan (350°F), Gas Mark 4.

2 Place the tortilla triangles in a bowl, drizzle or spray with about 2 tablespoons of olive oil and sprinkle with 2 teaspoons of paprika, ½ teaspoon of salt and a pinch of pepper, and toss to coat them evenly.

3 Arrange them in a single layer in the air fryer basket or on a baking tray and air fry or bake for 6–8 minutes, flipping halfway, until golden and crisp.

4 Leave them to cool for a few minutes – they'll crisp up even more as they sit.

TIP

Add some cayenne pepper too if you like a little heat. Serve with Classic Chunky Guacamole and Homemade Fresh Salsa (see opposite).

pictured overleaf

Classic Chunky Guacamole

Creamy avocado with chunky tomato, onion and lime. Simple, fresh and
the kind of guac you'll be eating straight from the bowl.

INGREDIENTS:

1 large ripe avocado, halved

½ small red onion, finely chopped

1 tomato, finely chopped

1 garlic clove, crushed

Juice of ½ lime

Small handful of chopped coriander

STAPLE INGREDIENTS:

Salt

Pepper

1 Scoop the avocado flesh into a bowl and mash with a fork until mostly smooth, but still slightly chunky.

2 Add the onion, tomato, garlic, lime juice and coriander. Season with salt and pepper, then mix everything together until well combined. Taste it and adjust the lime and seasoning if needed.

3 Serve immediately or cover tightly with clingfilm pressed directly onto the surface to prevent browning. It will stay fresh for 1–2 days in the refrigerator, but it's best eaten the day it's made.

Homemade Fresh Salsa

Zesty, fresh and perfect for dipping, this salsa is miles better than anything from a jar.
Great with chips, tacos or spooned over grilled chicken.

INGREDIENTS:

3 ripe tomatoes, finely chopped

½ small red onion, finely chopped

1 garlic glove, crushed, or 1 teaspoon
   garlic purée

Small handful of chopped coriander

Juice of 1 lime

STAPLE INGREDIENTS:

Salt

Pepper

1 Place the tomato, onion, garlic and coriander in a bowl. Squeeze over the lime juice, season with salt and pepper, and mix well to combine.

2 Serve straight away or chill in the refrigerator for 20–30 minutes to let the flavours come together.

3 Store in an airtight container in the refrigerator for up to 2–3 days.

pictured overleaf

Mini Caramelized Onion Sausage Rolls

Buttery puff pastry is wrapped around sausage filling with a sweet onion twist. These little rolls are so moreish and perfect for snacking or parties.

INGREDIENTS:

1 sheet of ready-rolled puff pastry, about 320g (11¼oz)

4 tablespoons caramelized onion jam or chutney

250g (9oz) sausagemeat or sausages, skinned

1 egg, beaten

STAPLE INGREDIENTS:

Salt

Pepper

1 Remove the puff pastry from the refrigerator and leave at room temperature for 5–10 minutes so it's easier to unroll.

2 Preheat your oven to 200°C, 180°C fan (400°F), Gas Mark 6 and line a baking tray with baking paper.

3 Unroll the puff pastry and cut it in half lengthways.

4 Spread a thin layer of caramelized onion jam lengthways down the centre of each rectangle. Place a line of sausagemeat on top of the chutney and season lightly with salt and pepper.

5 Brush one long edge of each strip of pastry with a little beaten egg, then roll the pastry over the sausagemeat to enclose it, pressing the edges together to seal.

6 Turn the rolls over so they are seam side down and cut each long roll into bite-sized pieces, about 6–8 per roll.

7 Arrange them on the lined baking tray, brush the tops with more beaten egg and make 2 cuts through the pastry in the top of each mini roll to let the steam escape.

8 Bake for 20–25 minutes, until puffed and golden, and the sausage is cooked through. Serve warm or cold.

9 They can be stored in an airtight container in the refrigerator for up to 3 days (let them cool fully before refrigerating so they don't go soggy).

Sticky Glazed Meatballs

These juicy meatballs coated in a sticky, glossy glaze are great as a party nibble or can be piled on rice, stuffed in sandwiches or served with spaghetti and sauce!

INGREDIENTS:

250g (9oz) minced beef or pork

½ egg

2 tablespoons breadcrumbs

1 garlic clove, crushed

2 tablespoons tomato ketchup

1½ tablespoons honey

STAPLE INGREDIENTS:

Salt

Pepper

Neutral oil, such as rapeseed

1   In a bowl, mix together the minced meat, egg, breadcrumbs, garlic and a good pinch of salt and pepper until just combined. Don't overwork the mixture. Roll the meat into 10 meatballs.

2   Heat a little oil in a frying pan over medium heat. Cook the meatballs for 10–12 minutes, turning frequently, until browned on all sides and cooked through.

3   In a small bowl, mix together the ketchup and honey to make a glaze.

4   Reduce the heat to low, pour the glaze into the pan and toss the meatballs until they're coated and sticky. This should take 1–2 minutes. Serve hot as a starter or tapas dish.

TIP

If you want to serve these meatballs in a pasta dish, such as the Sunday Night Spaghetti & Meatballs on page 87, follow Steps 1 and 2 of this recipe, then add the meatballs to your pasta sauce as usual.

Fresh Tomato Baguette

A crispy baguette topped with juicy tomato, garlic, olive oil and fresh basil.
Simple, rustic and packed with flavour.

INGREDIENTS:

½ large or 1 small baguette

2 ripe tomatoes

1 garlic clove, peeled

Small handful of basil leaves, torn

STAPLE INGREDIENTS:

Salt

Pepper

Olive oil

1 Slice the baguette into 2.5-cm (1-inch) pieces and toast lightly under the grill or in a hot pan until golden and crisp.

2 Meanwhile, cut the tomatoes in half, grate the cut sides on the coarse side of a grater, then discard the skins. You'll be left with a lovely fresh tomato pulp.

3 Rub one side of each piece of the toasted bread with the garlic clove for a subtle flavour.

4 Spoon the tomato pulp evenly over the warm bread and drizzle with about 1 tablespoon of olive oil. Season with salt and pepper.

5 Scatter with torn basil leaves to finish and serve immediately while crisp and fresh.

Garlic Bread & Pizza Baguette

Half pizza, half garlic bread and totally delicious. This 2-in-1 dish is quick to throw together and always a crowd-pleaser. Cut it into small pieces or keep it to yourself, we don't judge around here.

INGREDIENTS:

1 small baguette

2–3 tablespoons pizza sauce

50g (1¾oz) mozzarella cheese, grated

20g (¾oz) salted butter, softened

2 garlic cloves, crushed, or 2 teaspoons garlic purée

1 tablespoon finely chopped parsley

1   Preheat your oven to 200°C, 180°C fan (400°F), Gas Mark 6 or your air fryer to 180°C (350°F).

2   Spilt the baguette: one half will be used for the pizza and the other for the garlic bread.

3   For the pizza: Spread the pizza sauce evenly over the cut side of the baguette and top with the mozzarella cheese.

4   For the garlic bread: In a small bowl, mix the softened butter with the garlic and parsley. Spread it over the other piece of baguette.

5   Place both baguette halves on a baking tray or in the air fryer basket. Cook for 12–15 minutes in the oven or 8–10 minutes in the air fryer until golden and crisp. The garlic bread may need slightly less time, so if you like it softer, put it in a few minutes later than the pizza.

6   Slice and serve hot.

TIP

You could add extra toppings to the pizza, such as pepperoni or a pinch of dried Italian herbs.

Bakes & Cakes

CHOCOLATE BUTTON SHORTBREAD 148

CINNAMON APPLE CRUMBLE 150

VICTORIA SPONGE CAKE JARS 152

LEMON DRIZZLE LOAF CAKE 154

CHOCOLATE SCHOOL CAKE 156

LEMON BLUEBERRY YOGURT CAKE 158

MOIST BANANA BREAD 160

WHITE CHOCOLATE BLACKCURRANT FLAPJACKS 162

LEMON CREAM PUFFS 164

PEACHES & CREAM DANISHES 166

SOFT & CHEWY CHOCOLATE COOKIES 168

CHOCOLATE CHIP MUFFINS 170

RASPBERRY CRUMBLE BARS 172

COOKIES & CREAM CAKE 174

PEACH UPSIDE DOWN CAKE 176

CHOCOLATE CARAMEL BLONDIES 178

SEASONAL SUGAR COOKIES 180

Makes 16 · Prep time: 10 minutes · Cooking time: 20–25 minutes

Chocolate Button Shortbread

These soft, buttery shortbread squares are packed with chocolate buttons and sprinkled with sugar. A bakery favourite that's super easy to make and guaranteed to please.

INGREDIENTS:

225g (8oz) unsalted butter, softened
115g (4oz) granulated sugar, plus extra
   for sprinkling
320g (11¼oz) plain flour
180g (6¼oz) giant chocolate buttons

STAPLE INGREDIENTS:

Salt (optional)

1   Preheat your oven to 180°C, 160°C fan (350°F), Gas Mark 4 and line a 20cm (8 inch) square tin with baking paper, leaving some overhang for easy removal.

2   In a bowl, use your hands to mix together the softened butter, sugar, flour and ½ teaspoon of salt, if using, until fully combined and crumbly.

3   Fold through the chocolate buttons until evenly distributed.

4   Transfer the dough to your lined tin and press it down with the back of a spoon to make an even layer.

5   Sprinkle the surface with extra granulated sugar and bake in the oven for 20–25 minutes until pale golden on top and just set in the middle.

6   Remove from the oven and leave to cool completely in the tin before lifting out and slicing into 16 squares.

7   Store at room temperature in an airtight container for up to 1 week.

Cinnamon Apple Crumble

Warm cinnamon apples topped with a buttery crumble topping, this is the ultimate comfort dessert and one that really reminds me of home.

INGREDIENTS:

6 apples (about 900g/2lb), peeled, cored and sliced (I use a mix of Bramley and Jazz apples)

100g (3½oz) light soft brown sugar

2 teaspoons ground cinnamon

100g (3½oz) unsalted butter, chilled and cubed

100g (3½oz) caster sugar

150g (5½oz) plain flour

STAPLE INGREDIENTS:

Salt (optional)

1 Preheat your oven to 180°C, 160°C fan (350°F), Gas Mark 4.

2 Place the sliced apples in a large ovenproof dish, about 25 x 30cm (10 x 12 inches), sprinkle with the light soft brown sugar and the cinnamon, and toss to coat them evenly.

3 For the crumble topping, put the butter, caster sugar, flour and a pinch of salt (if using) into a large bowl, then rub together with your fingertips until the mixture resembles coarse breadcrumbs.

4 Spread the crumble topping evenly over the apples, covering them completely.

5 Bake for 40–45 minutes or until the top is golden brown and the apples are bubbling underneath. Serve warm or cold.

6 Cover and store any leftovers in the refrigerator for up to 3 days.

TIP

Serve the crumble with cream, custard or ice cream.

Victoria Sponge Cake Jars

Classic sponge cake layered with jam and cream – perfect for picnics, parties or whenever you want cake on the go. Because who doesn't want cake on the go?

INGREDIENTS:

100g (3½oz) salted butter or margarine, softened
100g (3½oz) caster sugar
100g (3½oz) self-raising flour
2 eggs, at room temperature
300ml (10fl oz) double cream, chilled
100g (3½oz) strawberry or raspberry jam

1 Preheat your oven to 180°C, 160°C fan (350°F), Gas Mark 4 and line a 20cm (8 inch) square tin with baking paper, leaving some overhang for easy removal.

2 Put the butter or margarine, sugar, flour and eggs into a large mixing bowl, and beat with an electric whisk until combined.

3 Spread the batter evenly in the tin and bake for 17–20 minutes until golden and springy to the touch, then let it cool fully in the tin.

4 In a clean bowl, whip the double cream to soft peaks.

5 Break the cooled sponge into chunks.

6 Place a layer of sponge in the bottoms of 4 jars, add 1–2 spoonfuls of jam and a layer of whipped cream, then repeat until the jars are full.

7 Finish with a swirl of cream and a little spoonful of jam on top.

8 Best eaten fresh on the day, but they'll keep covered in the refrigerator for up to 24 hours.

TIPS

Add a little icing sugar or vanilla extract to the cream if you wish to make it sweeter.

Feel free to add some fresh strawberries or raspberries for decoration.

Lemon Drizzle Loaf Cake

This zingy lemon loaf cake is topped with a tangy drizzle and a thick layer of lemon icing. It's fresh, moist and light – perfect with a cup of tea.

INGREDIENTS:

225g (8oz) salted butter or margarine, softened
225g (8oz) caster sugar
4 large eggs, at room temperature
225g (8oz) self-raising flour
Finely grated zest of 1 lemon, plus 4 tablespoons juice
200g (7oz) icing sugar

1   Preheat your oven to 180°C, 160°C fan (350°F), Gas Mark 4 and line a 900g (2lb) loaf tin with baking paper.

2   In a large bowl, beat the butter or margarine and caster sugar with an electric whisk until pale and fluffy.

3   Add the eggs and flour, and whisk until just combined, then fold in the lemon zest.

4   Scoop the batter into your prepared loaf tin and smooth the top. Bake for 45–55 minutes until golden and a toothpick inserted in the centre comes out with a few moist crumbs.

5   When the cake has about 5 minutes left, make the drizzle. Mix 50g (1¾oz) of the icing sugar with 3 tablespoons of the lemon juice in a bowl until smooth.

6   While the cake is still warm in the tin, poke holes into it about three-quarters of the way down with a skewer. Pour the drizzle evenly over the cake so it seeps into the holes. Let it cool fully in the tin.

7   For the glaze, mix the remaining icing sugar with the remaining lemon juice and 1 tablespoon of water in a bowl until smooth and pourable, but thick. Add more icing sugar if needed.

8   Remove the cooled cake from the tin and place it on a wire rack. Pour the glaze over the top, letting it drip down the sides slightly. For a thicker glaze, let one layer set, then pour over a second layer.

9   Store in an airtight container at room temperature for up to 4 days.

Serves 9–16 · Prep time: 10 minutes · Cooking time: 30–40 minutes

Chocolate School Cake

A nostalgic traybake topped with chocolatey icing and sprinkles.
Simple, old-school and super easy to make.

INGREDIENTS:

225g (8oz) margarine or salted butter,
    softened
225g (8oz) caster sugar
185g (6½oz) self-raising flour
40g (1½oz) cocoa powder
4 large eggs, at room temperature
175g (6oz) icing sugar, sifted

1   Preheat the oven to 170°C, 150°C fan (335°F), Gas Mark 3½. Line a 20cm (8 inch) square tin with baking paper.

2   In a large bowl, beat the margarine or butter and caster sugar together until pale and fluffy.

3   Add the flour, 25g (1oz) of the cocoa powder and the eggs. Whisk until just combined (don't overmix).

4   Pour the batter into your prepared tin and smooth it out evenly. Bake for 30–40 minutes, or until a toothpick inserted into the middle comes out with a few moist crumbs. Leave to cool.

5   For the icing, put the icing sugar and remaining cocoa powder into a medium bowl, then 2–3 tablespoons of boiling water, a tablespoon at a time, stirring well each time, until smooth and spreadable.

6   Pour the icing evenly over the cooled cake. Allow to set at room temperature before slicing into 9 or 16 squares. Enjoy!

7   Store in an airtight container for up to 3 days.

TIP

You could decorate this cake with chocolate sprinkles or chocolate shavings, or just leave it plain.

Lemon Blueberry Yogurt Cake

This soft and fluffy cake is made with yogurt for extra moisture, and dotted with blueberries and zesty lemon. Ideal for a spring or summer celebration.

INGREDIENTS:

2 large eggs, at room temperature

200ml (7fl oz) 5% fat Greek yogurt

Finely grated zest of 1 lemon

200g (7oz) self-raising flour

150g (5½oz) caster sugar

150g (5½oz) fresh or frozen blueberries

STAPLE INGREDIENTS:

Salt

Neutral oil, such as rapeseed

1 Preheat your oven to 180°C, 160°C fan (350°F), Gas Mark 4 and line a 20cm (8 inch) square tin with baking paper, leaving some overhang for easy removal.

2 In a large bowl, beat together the eggs, yogurt, 100ml (3½fl oz) of oil and the lemon zest with an electric whisk until smooth.

3 Stir in the flour, sugar and ½ teaspoon of salt using a rubber spatula until just combined. Don't overmix – a few lumps are fine.

4 If using fresh blueberries, gently fold them into the batter, then pour the batter into your prepared tin and spread it evenly. If using frozen, sprinkle them on top after spreading the batter in the tin.

5 Bake for 25–30 minutes or until the top is lightly golden and a toothpick inserted in the centre comes out with a few moist crumbs.

6 Allow to cool in the tin for 10 minutes, then lift out and cool completely on a wire rack. Slice into 9 or 16 squares.

7 The cake can be stored in an airtight container for up to 3 days.

TIP

You can dust the cake with icing sugar or glaze with icing once cooled.

Serves 8–10 · Prep time: 10 minutes · Cooking time: 45–55 minutes

Moist Banana Bread

Great for using up overripe bananas, this soft and perfectly moist banana bread is the kind you'll want to slice thickly and spread with butter.

INGREDIENTS:

4 ripe bananas (about 350g/12oz peeled weight)
2 large eggs
130g (4¾oz) soft light brown sugar
160g (5¾oz) self-raising flour
2 teaspoons ground cinnamon

STAPLE INGREDIENTS:

Salt
Neutral oil, such as rapeseed

1 Preheat your oven to 180°C, 160°C fan (350°F), Gas Mark 4 and line a 900g (2lb) loaf tin with baking paper.

2 In a large bowl, mash the bananas until smooth using a fork. Whisk in the eggs, sugar and 80ml (2¾fl oz) of oil until combined.

3 Sift in the flour, cinnamon and 1 teaspoon of salt, then fold these in gently until just combined (don't overmix).

4 Pour the batter into the prepared tin and smooth the top. Bake for 45–55 minutes or until a toothpick inserted in the centre comes out with a few moist crumbs.

5 Allow to cool in the tin for 10 minutes, then transfer to a wire rack. Serve warm or at room temperature.

6 Store in an airtight container for up to 4 days.

White Chocolate Blackcurrant Flapjacks

Drizzled with white chocolate and swirled with tangy blackcurrant jam,
these are a little bit fruity, a little bit indulgent and just so good.

INGREDIENTS:

150g (5½oz) unsalted butter

120g (4¼oz) soft light brown sugar

80ml (2¾fl oz) honey

280g (10oz) rolled oats

250g (9oz) white chocolate

100g (3½oz) blackcurrant jam

1 Preheat your oven to 180°C, 160°C fan (350°F), Gas Mark 4 and line a 20cm (8 inch) square tin with baking paper, leaving some overhang for easy removal.

2 Melt the butter, sugar and honey in a saucepan over medium-low heat, stirring constantly until smooth.

3 Remove from the heat, then stir in the oats until they're fully coated. Scoop the mixture into your prepared tin and press down evenly.

4 Bake for 20 minutes or until the edges are golden. It should still wobble in the middle – this is the key to soft and chewy flapjacks. Leave to cool completely in the tin.

5 Melt the white chocolate in the microwave on medium heat in 1 minute bursts, stirring each time until smooth. Pour it over the cooled flapjack and spread evenly.

6 Warm the blackcurrant jam in the microwave for 10–15 seconds to loosen it.

7 Dollop spoonfuls of jam over the melted chocolate, then use a skewer or knife to swirl it through for a marbled effect.

8 Allow the topping to set at room temperature before slicing into 9 or 16 squares.

9 Store in an airtight container at room temperature for up to 5 days.

Makes 10 · Prep time: 10 minutes · Cooking time: 10 minutes

Lemon Cream Puffs

These flaky puff pastry slices are baked, then filled with a lemon cream and lemon curd. They're light and zesty, and look much fancier than the effort it takes to make them.

INGREDIENTS:

1 sheet of ready-rolled puff pastry, about 320g (11¼oz)

1 small egg

250ml (9fl oz) double cream

30g (1oz) icing sugar, plus extra for dusting

Finely grated zest of 1 lemon, plus 1 tablespoon juice

150g (5½oz) lemon curd

1. Remove the puff pastry from the refrigerator and leave at room temperature for 5–10 minutes so that it's easier to unroll.

2. Preheat your oven to 200°C, 180°C fan (400°F), Gas Mark 6 and line a large baking tray with baking paper.

3. Unroll the puff pastry and cut it in half lengthways, then cut each half into 5 equal rectangles to make 10 in total. Transfer the pastry rectangles to the lined baking tray, arranging them about 2.5cm (1 inch) apart.

4. Beat the egg with 1 teaspoon of water until combined to make an egg wash, then brush it over the pastries. Bake for 10 minutes until puffed and golden, then leave to cool on the baking tray.

5. Once cooled, split them open using a serrated knife.

6. In a large mixing bowl, whisk the cream, icing sugar and lemon juice until thick. Transfer to a piping bag fitted with a large open star nozzle.

7. Pipe or spread lemon curd over the bottom halves of the pastries, then pipe on the lemon cream and sprinkle with the lemon zest. Place the pastry lids carefully back on top.

8. Dust with icing sugar and serve straight away. They are best served fresh, on the day they are made.

Peaches & Cream Danishes

The perfect quick and easy summer pastry. They're fresh and fruity, smooth and creamy, and the flaky golden pastry ties it all together. Super simple to make at home and guaranteed to please!

INGREDIENTS:

120g (4¼oz) cream cheese, softened

30g (1oz) icing sugar

1 sheet of ready-rolled puff pastry, about 320g (11¼oz)

8 teaspoons peach or apricot jam

2 peaches, thinly sliced

1 small egg, beaten

1 Remove the puff pastry from the refrigerator and leave at room temperature for 5–10 minutes so that it's easier to unroll.

2 Preheat your oven to 200°C, 180°C fan (400°F), Gas Mark 6 and line a large baking tray with baking paper.

3 In a small mixing bowl, beat the cream cheese and icing sugar together with an electric whisk until smooth and creamy, then set aside.

4 Unroll the puff pastry and cut it in half lengthways, then cut each half into 4 equal rectangles to make 8 in total. Transfer the rectangles of pastry to the lined baking tray, arranging them about 2.5cm (1 inch) apart.

5 Score a 1cm (½ inch) border around each rectangle with a sharp knife, making sure you don't cut all the way through.

6 Spread 1 tablespoon of the cream cheese mixture on each rectangle, staying inside the border. Then add 1 teaspoon of jam and spread it in a line down the middle.

7 Arrange 4–5 peach slices on top of each pastry rectangle, slightly overlapping them.

8 Use a pastry brush to coat the pastry borders with beaten egg to create a golden, glossy finish.

9 Bake for 10–12 minutes until crisp and golden brown.

10 Store in an airtight container in the refrigerator for up to 3 days. The pastries are best served fresh on the day they are made, warm or cold.

TIP

You can drizzle the pastries with icing for extra sweetness. Just mix 50g (1¾oz) of icing sugar with ½ tablespoon of milk or water.

Makes 6 · Prep time: 10 minutes · Cooking time: 10 minutes

Soft & Chewy Chocolate Cookies

Soft and chewy cookies made with chocolate hazelnut spread. So easy to make and guaranteed to please any chocolate lover.

INGREDIENTS:

300g (10½oz) chocolate hazelnut spread (I use Nutella)

85g (3oz) plain flour, sifted

1 large egg, at room temperature

1 teaspoon baking powder

150g (5½oz) chocolate chips or chunks of your choice

1   Preheat your oven to 200°C, 180°C fan (400°F), Gas Mark 6 and line a large baking tray with baking paper.

2   In a large bowl, mix together the chocolate hazelnut spread, flour, egg and baking powder with a rubber spatula until fully combined. You should have a thick cookie dough texture. Fold in the chocolate chips or chunks until evenly distributed.

3   Divide the dough into 6 equal balls (about 1 heaped tablespoon each) and arrange them on the lined baking tray at least 10cm (4 inches) apart. You may need 2 baking trays or to cook them in batches.

4   Bake for 10 minutes or until the edges are crisp, but the middles still look puffy.

5   Allow to cool for at least 15 minutes on the tray before trying to move them.

6   Store in an airtight container at room temperature for up to 4 days.

TIP

Feel free to swap the chocolate hazelnut spread for regular chocolate spread if preferred.

Chocolate Chip Muffins

Tall, fluffy muffins packed with melty chocolate chips. They're a classic bake that are perfect for any time of the day.

INGREDIENTS:

2 large eggs, at room temperature

120ml (3¾fl oz) milk (any)

1 teaspoon vanilla extract

250g (9oz) self-raising flour

200g (7oz) caster sugar

80g (2¾oz) chocolate chips or chunks, plus extra for sprinkling

STAPLE INGREDIENTS:

Neutral oil, such as rapeseed

1 In a large mixing bowl, whisk the eggs, 4 tablespoons of oil, the milk and vanilla extract together until fully combined.

2 In another large mixing bowl, use a balloon whisk to whisk the flour and sugar until combined.

3 Pour the wet ingredients into the dry ingredients and fold them together using a rubber spatula until just mixed. The batter should be nice and thick. Try not to overmix as this can lead to tougher, denser muffins.

4 Fold in the chocolate, again trying not to overmix. Cover the bowl with cling film and chill in the refrigerator for 1 hour.

5 Preheat your oven to 220°C, 200°C fan (425°F), Gas Mark 7 and line 8 holes of a muffin tin with muffin cases.

6 Scoop the mixture into your muffin cases, about three-quarters full, smooth them out evenly, then sprinkle with extra chocolate chips.

7 Bake for 7 minutes, then turn the heat down to 190°C, 170°C fan (375°F), Gas Mark 5 and bake for a further 13 minutes, until the tops are golden brown and a toothpick inserted in the centre comes out with a few moist crumbs. Don't open the oven while the muffins are baking.

8 Leave to cool in the tin for 10–15 minutes before eating.

9 Store in an airtight container at room temperature for up to 4 days.

Raspberry Crumble Bars

These buttery crumble bars are layered with a fruity raspberry filling and are perfect with a cup of tea. They could be made with other fruits and jams – try blackberries and blackberry jam, strawberries and strawberry jam or apricots and apricot jam if you prefer.

INGREDIENTS:

225g (8oz) salted butter, softened
1 320g (11¼oz) plain flour
80g (6¼oz) granulated sugar
230g (8¼oz) frozen raspberries
150g (5½oz) raspberry jam
3 tablespoons cornflour

1   Preheat your oven to 190°C, 170°C fan (375°F), Gas Mark 5 and line a 20cm (8 inch) square tin with baking paper, leaving some overhang for easy removal.

2   In a large bowl, mix the butter with the flour and 120g (4¼oz) of the sugar until the mixture is combined and crumbly.

3   Press half this shortbread mixture into your prepared tin and smooth down firmly with the back of a spoon. Bake for 15 minutes, then allow to cool fully in the tin.

4   In a large bowl, combine the frozen raspberries, raspberry jam, remaining sugar and the cornflour. Mix well until it forms a thick, bright red mixture.

5   Spread the raspberry filling evenly over the cooled base, then crumble the remaining shortbread mixture evenly over the top.

6   Return to the oven and bake for 35 minutes or until golden on top and bubbling around the edges.

7   Allow to cool completely in the tin then slice into 16 squares.

8   Store in an airtight container for up to 2 days or in the refrigerator for 4–5 days (this helps them to stay firmer).

Serves 16 · Prep time: 10 minutes · Cooking time: 20–25 minutes

Cookies & Cream Cake

This moist chocolate sponge is made with just three ingredients:
cookies, baking powder and milk. Then topped with a thick layer
of cream cheese frosting. It's perfect with a hot drink.

INGREDIENTS:

45 cookies and cream biscuits
(about 500g/1lb 2oz; I use Oreos),
plus extra for sprinkling (optional)
1½ teaspoons baking powder
380ml (13¼fl oz) milk (any), at room
temperature
45g (1½oz) unsalted butter, softened
45g (1½oz) cream cheese, at room
temperature
125g (4½oz) icing sugar, sifted

1 Preheat your oven to 180°C, 160°C fan (350°F), Gas Mark 4 and line a 20cm (8 inch) square tin with baking paper, leaving some overhang for easy removal.

2 Twist the cookies apart and scrape out the cream filling into a small bowl, then set it aside.

3 Crush the cookies into fine crumbs using a food processor or by placing them in a plastic bag and bashing them with a rolling pin.

4 In a large bowl, whisk together the cookie crumbs and baking powder. Pour in the milk and whisk until smooth.

5 Add the cream filling and whisk again until combined, then pour the mixture into your prepared tin.

6 Bake for 20–25 minutes or until a toothpick inserted comes out with a few moist crumbs. Leave to cool completely.

7 In a large bowl, beat the softened butter and cream cheese together until smooth, then gradually add the icing sugar and whisk until smooth and thick (try not to overmix).

8 Remove the cake from the tin and spread the frosting evenly over the cooled cake. Sprinkle with extra cookie crumbs if desired.

9 Store in an airtight container in the refrigerator for up to 3 days. Bring to room temperate before serving for the best texture.

Peach Upside Down Cake

Juicy peaches are baked into a golden caramel topping with soft sponge underneath.
This is a peachy twist on the classic pineapple version.

INGREDIENTS:

260g (9½oz) salted butter, softened

120g (4¼oz) soft light brown sugar

3 ripe peaches

200g (7oz) caster sugar

3 large eggs, at room temperature

200g (7oz) self-raising flour

1 Preheat your oven to 180°C, 160°C fan (350°F), Gas Mark 4 and line a 23cm (9 inch) round cake tin with baking paper (if using a loose-bottomed tin, line the whole tin to prevent leaks).

2 Melt 60g (2¼oz) of the butter and pour it into the base of the tin, then sprinkle over the brown sugar.

3 Slice the peaches into 5mm (¼ inch) thick slices and arrange them neatly over the sugar layer.

4 In a bowl, beat together the remaining butter with the caster sugar until pale and fluffy.

5 Add the eggs one at a time, whisking well after each addition. Fold in the self-raising flour until just combined (try not to overmix).

6 Spoon the batter gently over the peaches, spreading evenly, then bake for 35–40 minutes or until golden and a toothpick inserted in the centre comes out with a few moist crumbs.

7 Let it cool in the tin for 5 minutes, then carefully flip it out onto a serving plate while still warm.

8 Peel off the paper to reveal the caramelized peach topping. Slice it up and enjoy!

9 Best served warm on the day it is baked but it will keep for up to 2 days in an airtight container.

Chocolate Caramel Blondies

These sweet and fudgy white chocolate blondies are packed with chunks of caramel-filled chocolate. Chewy and indulgent, you'll want to make these again and again.

INGREDIENTS:

115g (4oz) unsalted butter

225g (8oz) white chocolate, broken into chunks

2 large eggs

70g (2½oz) granulated sugar

155g (5¾oz) plain flour

180g (6¼oz) caramel-filled milk chocolate, broken into pieces

STAPLE INGREDIENTS:

Salt

TIP

For extra fudginess, chill them in the refrigerator for about an hour before slicing.

1   Preheat your oven to 170°C, 150°C fan (340°F), Gas Mark 3½ and line a 20cm (8 inch) square tin with baking paper, leaving some overhang for easy removal.

2   Heat the butter and white chocolate in the microwave on low to medium, stirring every 20–30 seconds, until fully melted and smooth. Make sure you don't overheat the mixture otherwise it can burn or turn lumpy. Set aside to cool.

3   In a large mixing bowl, beat the eggs until light and frothy using an electric whisk, then add the sugar and whisk until combined.

4   Pour in the melted butter and white chocolate mixture and stir until smooth.

5   Sift in the flour and ½ teaspoon of salt, then fold in until just combined (try not to overmix).

6   Gently fold in the chocolate chunks so they're well distributed, then pour the batter into the prepared tin, spreading it out evenly.

7   Bake for 25–30 minutes, or until the top is crisp and light golden brown. The centre should no longer wobble, but it should be slightly soft – it will set as it cools. Don't overbake or the blondies will become cakey.

8   Allow the blondies to cool fully in the tin, then cut into 9 or 16 pieces.

9   Store in an airtight container at room temperature or in the refrigerator for up to 4 days.

Seasonal Sugar Cookies

Easy to adapt and fun to decorate with friends or family, these crisp, buttery sugar cookies are perfect for any occasion, from Halloween or Christmas to Easter or Diwali.

INGREDIENTS:

225g (8oz) salted butter, softened

150g (5½oz) granulated sugar

1 egg

400g (14oz) plain flour, plus extra
   for dusting

¼ teaspoon baking powder

220g (7¾oz) icing sugar

1. Preheat your oven to 180°C, 160°C fan (350°F), Gas Mark 4 and line a large baking tray with baking paper.

2. In a large bowl, beat the butter and sugar until pale and fluffy, then whisk in the egg until combined.

3. Sift in the flour and baking powder, and fold these in with your hands to form a sturdy dough.

4. Dust your surface and rolling pin with flour, then roll out the dough to 5mm (¼ inch) thick.

5. Cut out shapes using your favourite cookie cutters, then remove any excess dough and roll it out again to create more shapes.

6. Carefully transfer the shapes to the lined baking tray and bake for 5–6 minutes until they're golden, but no longer or they'll turn hard and crunchy. Leave to cool on the baking tray before trying to move them, so they don't break.

7. If making the icing (optional), put the icing sugar in a small bowl and gradually add 4–5 tablespoons of hot water, a spoonful at a time, stirring until smooth and thick.

8. Pour over the cooled cookies on a wire rack or dip them into the icing. Allow the icing to set at room temperature.

9. Store in an airtight container for up to 4 days.

TIP

Add food colouring
to the icing to suit
your theme.

No-Bake Desserts

LEMON TIRAMISU 184

BANOFFEE PIE 186

SALTED CHOCOLATE TART 188

NO-CHURN PISTACHIO ICE CREAM 190

ONE-POT SPECULOOS CHEESECAKE 192

SALTED CARAMEL CHEESECAKE BARS 194

ULTIMATE CHOCOLATE CHEESECAKE 196

BLUEBERRY CHEESECAKE 200

BEST VANILLA CHEESECAKE 201

ONE-POT LEMON CHEESECAKE 202

SPECULOOS CORNFLAKES BARS 204

WHITE CHOCOLATE HAZELNUT BISCUIT BARS 206

MINI EASTER EGG CHEESECAKES 208

THICK ITALIAN-STYLE HOT CHOCOLATE 210

BIRTHDAY CAKE FUDGE 212

EASY CLASSIC TIRAMISU 214

CHOCOLATE HAZELNUT FINGERS 216

BROWN BUTTER TOASTED MARSHMALLOW CRISPIES 218

Lemon Tiramisu

A lemony twist on classic tiramisu. Layers of zesty cream, tangy lemon curd and sponge fingers come together for a dessert that's light, fresh and super delicious.

INGREDIENTS:

350ml (12fl oz) double cream, chilled

70g (2½oz) icing sugar

Finely grated zest of 1 lemon, plus
   5 tablespoons juice

26 sponge fingers

320g (11¼oz) lemon curd

1 First make the lemon cream. In a large bowl, whisk the double cream with 50g (1¾oz) of the icing sugar, the lemon zest and 1 tablespoon of the lemon juice to soft peaks. Be careful not to overwhip – the mixture should be smooth and spreadable.

2 Next make the lemon syrup. Whisk together the remaining lemon juice and the remaining icing sugar until dissolved.

3 Quickly dip half the sponge fingers, one at a time, into the lemon syrup and arrange them in a single layer across the bottom of a 15 x 25cm (6 x 10 inch) serving dish. Don't soak them otherwise they can go soggy.

4 Spread half the lemon cream evenly over the top.

5 Spread half the lemon curd evenly over the cream. You might need to whisk the lemon curd for a minute or two to loosen it before spreading.

6 Repeat the layers, finishing with the remaining lemon curd, and smooth it out nice and evenly.

7 Cover and chill in the refrigerator for at least 6 hours (or overnight) to allow the flavours to come together.

8 Cover with clingfilm and store in the refrigerator for up to 3 days.

TIP

Just before serving, you could decorate the tiramisu with lemon slices and a few fresh mint leaves in the corners if you like.

Banoffee Pie

Sweet bananas, silky caramel and plenty of whipped cream all piled onto a salty biscuit base. This is my favourite dessert of all time.

INGREDIENTS:

250g (9oz) digestive biscuits

125g (4½oz) salted butter, melted

400g (14oz) can caramel or
    dulce de leche

2 large bananas, sliced

300ml (10fl oz) double cream, chilled

2 tablespoons icing sugar

1 For the base, crush the digestive biscuits into fine crumbs using a food processor or place them in a plastic bag and crush with a rolling pin.

2 Pour the crumbs into a bowl and mix them with the melted butter until evenly coated.

3 Press the mixture firmly into the base of a 20cm (8 inch) dish or tin to form an even layer.

4 Spread the caramel evenly over the biscuit base, then arrange the banana slices in an even layer over the caramel.

5 In a large bowl, whisk the double cream and icing sugar to soft peaks, then spread or pipe the whipped cream gently over the bananas.

6 Chill in the refrigerator for at least 1 hour before serving to allow the layers to firm up.

7 Keep it covered in the refrigerator (with clingfilm or in an airtight container) for 2–3 days. This is best eaten on day 1 or 2 as the bananas will start to brown.

TIP

Decorate your pie with chocolate shavings or cocoa powder for extra flavour if you like.

Salted Chocolate Tart

A rich, glossy chocolate filling with a hint of salt to balance the richness. It looks fancy enough for a posh dinner party, but it's actually really easy to make.

INGREDIENTS:

300g (10½oz) digestive biscuits

150g (5½oz) salted butter, melted

230g (8¼oz) dark chocolate, broken into pieces

280ml (9½fl oz) double cream

Flaky sea salt, for sprinkling

1 For the base, crush the digestive biscuits into fine crumbs using a food processor or place them in a plastic bag and crush with a rolling pin.

2 Pour the crumbs into a bowl and mix them with the melted butter until evenly coated.

3 Press the mixture firmly into the base and up the sides of a deep 20cm (8 inches) loose-bottom tart tin to form an even layer. Chill in the refrigerator while you make the filling.

4 Place the dark chocolate and cream in a microwave-safe bowl or jug. Microwave on medium heat for 1 minute 20 seconds, then let it sit for 1 minute. Stir gently until smooth and glossy.

5 Pour the chocolate filling into the chilled base and sprinkle the top with flaky sea salt.

6 Refrigerate for at least 4 hours (or overnight) until set. Use a hot knife (dipped in hot water and wiped dry) to slice into neat portions.

7 Store in the refrigerator for up to 3 days in an airtight container.

TIP

Chocolate with around 55% cocoa solids is the best choice for this tart.

No-Churn Pistachio Ice Cream

Creamy pistachio ice cream made without a machine — yay!
It's thick, rich, nutty and ridiculously easy to whip up at home.

INGREDIENTS:

400g (14oz) can sweetened condensed milk

475ml (17fl oz) double cream

250g (9oz) pistachio crème, plus extra to decorate (optional)

Chopped pistachios, to decorate (optional)

1 Put all the ingredients into a large mixing bowl and whisk until thick and fluffy.

2 Pour the ice cream into a 1 litre (1¾ pint) container or a 1.3kg (3lb) loaf tin. Smooth it out evenly if needed.

3 Cover and freeze for at least 6 hours (or overnight) until set.

4 Scoop straight from the freezer into bowls. Top with chopped pistachios or drizzle with melted pistachio crème for decoration.

TIP

Pistachio crème is also known as pistachio cream and is sold in jars as a spread.

One-Pot Speculoos Cheesecake

This is one of the most popular desserts on my social media! It's packed with Biscoff in every layer, from the buttery base to the creamy filling and that dreamy topping. It's super simple to make...the only challenge is waiting for it to set!

INGREDIENTS:

3 Biscoff or other speculoos cookies, plus extra to decorate

10g (¼oz) salted butter, melted

115g (4oz) cream cheese, at room temperature

1 tablespoon icing sugar

30g (1oz) Biscoff spread

1 For the base, crush the cookies into fine crumbs using a food processor or place them in a plastic bag and crush with a rolling pin.

2 Pour the crumbs into a bowl and mix them with the melted butter until evenly coated.

3 Press the mixture firmly into the base of 1 large ramekin or 2 small ones.

4 In a small bowl, beat the cream cheese, icing sugar and two-thirds of the Biscoff spread with an electric mixer until smooth and creamy. Make sure not to overmix, as it can turn runny.

5 Scoop the mixture into the ramekin(s) and smooth it out evenly.

6 Put the remaining Biscoff spread in a small microwave-safe bowl and microwave on low-medium heat for 20 seconds until melted. Pour it over the top of the cheesecake(s) and gently smooth it out.

7 Add half a Biscoff cookie on top for decoration, then refrigerate for at least 1 hour.

8 Store the cheesecake in an airtight container in the refrigerator for up to 3 days (if you can resist eating it immediately).

TIP

You can swap the Biscoff spread for another spread of your choice, such as peanut butter or Nutella.

Salted Caramel Cheesecake Bars

Easy no-bake cheesecake bars with a gooey salted caramel topping and buttery biscuit base — they're sweet, salty and so moreish.

INGREDIENTS:

250g (9oz) digestive biscuits

125g (4½oz) salted or unsalted butter, melted

500g (1lb 2oz) cream cheese, at room temperature

80g (2¾oz) icing sugar

300g (10½oz) thick salted caramel sauce

4 tablespoons fudge chunks

1 For the base, crush the biscuits into fine crumbs using a food processor or place them in a plastic bag and crush with a rolling pin.

2 Pour the crumbs into a bowl and mix them with the melted butter until evenly coated.

3 Press the mixture firmly into the base of a lined 20cm (8 inch) square tin and chill in the refrigerator while you make the filling.

4 In a large mixing bowl, beat the cream cheese, icing sugar and half the salted caramel sauce until smooth. Be careful not to overmix, as this can cause the filling to become runny and prevent it from setting properly.

5 Scoop the filling onto the chilled base and smooth it out.

6 Melt the remaining salted caramel sauce in the microwave for 20–30 seconds until it's smooth and pourable, then let it cool for a few minutes so it's not piping hot.

7 Gently pour it over the cheesecake, smoothing it out evenly. Chill for at least 4 hours (overnight is best).

8 Before serving, place little fudge chunks around the edge of the cheesecake to create a border. Slice into 16 squares and enjoy!

9 Store in an airtight container in the refrigerator for up to 3 days.

TIP

Use thick salted caramel sauce from a jar, not the canned variety. If you like a thicker topping, you can always add a second layer when the first layer has set.

Ultimate Chocolate Cheesecake

Rich, creamy and unapologetically chocolatey, this cheesecake is pure indulgence and guaranteed to wow anyone who is lucky enough to get a slice.

INGREDIENTS:

28 Oreo cookies (about 310g/11oz), plus extra to decorate
90g (3¼oz) salted butter, melted
460g (1lb 1oz) dark chocolate, broken into pieces
550ml (19fl oz) double cream, chilled
500g (1lb 2oz) cream cheese, at room temperature
120g (4¼oz) icing sugar

1 For the base, crush the cookies into fine crumbs using a food processor or place them in a plastic bag and crush with a rolling pin.

2 Pour the crumbs into a bowl and mix them with the melted butter until evenly coated.

3 Press the mixture firmly into the base of a lined 20cm (8 inch) springform tin and chill in the refrigerator while you make the filling.

4 Melt 200g (7oz) of the dark chocolate in the microwave on a medium heat in short bursts until melted and smooth, then leave to cool.

5 In a large bowl, whip 300ml (10fl oz) of the double cream to stiff peaks.

6 In another large bowl, beat the cream cheese, icing sugar and cooled melted chocolate until smooth and creamy. Gently fold in the whipped cream until just combined, but don't overmix.

7 Scoop the filling onto the chilled base, smooth the top and chill for at least 6 hours (overnight is best).

8 For the ganache topping, place the remaining dark chocolate and remaining double cream in a microwave-safe bowl or large jug. Microwave on a medium heat in bursts of 1½ minutes, stirring each time, until smooth and glossy. Let it cool slightly.

9   Remove the cheesecake from the tin and transfer to a serving plate. Pour half the ganache over the cheesecake in a smooth layer, letting it drip down the sides slightly.

10 Chill the cheesecake and the remaining ganache for about 2 hours until the ganache is firm enough to pipe.

11 Transfer the ganache to a piping bag fitted with a large star nozzle and pipe swirls around the edges of the cheesecake. Place cookie halves between the swirls to decorate.

12 Use a hot knife (dipped in hot water and wiped dry) to slice into neat portions.

13 Store in an airtight container in the refrigerator for up to 3 days.

TIP

Feel free to top with brownie chunks or your favourite chocolatey toppings to make it your own.

pictured overleaf

Blueberry Cheesecake

A creamy cheesecake swirled with juicy blueberries.
It's fruity, tangy and a real showstopper.

INGREDIENTS:

350g (12oz) shortbread biscuits

100g (3½oz) salted butter, melted

200g (7oz) blueberries, plus extra
   to decorate

500ml (18fl oz) double cream, chilled

500g (1lb 2oz) cream cheese, at room
   temperature

150g (5½oz) icing sugar

1 For the base, crush the biscuits into fine crumbs using a food processor or place them in a plastic bag and crush with a rolling pin.

2 Pour the crumbs into a bowl and mix them with the melted butter until evenly coated.

3 Press the mixture firmly into the base of a lined 20cm (8 inch) springform tin and chill in the refrigerator while you make the filling.

4 Place the blueberries in a microwave-safe bowl or large jug. Microwave on medium in bursts of 1 minute, stirring each time, until thick and jammy. Alternatively, put them in a small saucepan and cook on medium heat, stirring frequently. Set aside to cool completely (this is important).

5 In a large bowl, whip 350ml (12fl oz) of the double cream to stiff peaks.

6 In another large bowl, beat the cream cheese and icing sugar until smooth and creamy. Be careful not to overmix, as this can cause the filling to become runny and prevent it from setting properly. Gently fold in the whipped cream until just combined – don't overmix – then fold in the blueberries.

7 Scoop the filling onto the chilled base, smooth the top and chill for at least 6 hours (overnight is best).

8 Whip the remaining double cream to soft peaks. Transfer to a piping bag fitted with a large star nozzle and pipe swirls around the edge of the cheesecake. Top with fresh blueberries and enjoy!

9 Store in an airtight container in the refrigerator for up to 3 days.

pictured on pages 198–9

Best Vanilla Cheesecake

This classic, creamy vanilla cheesecake is silky smooth and never fails.
Simple, timeless and always delicious.

INGREDIENTS:

300g (10½oz) digestive biscuits
150g (5½oz) butter, melted
750ml (25fl oz) double cream, chilled
560g (1lb 4¼oz) cream cheese, at room temperature
120g (4¼oz) icing sugar
2 teaspoons vanilla extract

1 For the base, crush the biscuits into fine crumbs using a food processor or place them in a plastic bag and crush with a rolling pin.

2 Pour the crumbs into a bowl and mix them with the melted butter until evenly coated.

3 Press the mixture firmly into the base of a lined 20cm (8 inch) springform tin and chill in the refrigerator while you make the filling.

4 In a large bowl, whip 600ml (20fl oz) of the double cream to stiff peaks.

5 In another large bowl, beat the cream cheese, icing sugar and vanilla extract until smooth and creamy. Be careful not to overmix, as this can cause the filling to become runny and prevent it from setting properly. Gently fold in the whipped cream until just combined – don't overmix.

6 Scoop the filling onto the chilled base, smooth the top and chill for at least 6 hours (overnight is best).

7 Whip the remaining double cream to soft peaks. Transfer to a piping bag fitted with a large star nozzle and pipe swirls around the edge of the cheesecake.

8 Store in an airtight container in the refrigerator for up to 3 days.

TIP

Decorate this classic cheesecake with fresh berries, chocolate shavings or a drizzle of your favourite sauce for an extra touch.

pictured on pages 198–9

Serves 1–2 · Prep time: 10 minutes, plus chilling

⇒ One-Pot Lemon ⇐ Cheesecake

The perfect dessert when you don't want to whip up an entire cheesecake.
It's tangy, creamy and topped with zesty lemon curd.

INGREDIENTS:

2 shortbread biscuits

10g (¼oz) salted butter, melted

115g (4oz) cream cheese, at room temperature

1 tablespoon icing sugar

1 tablespoon lemon juice

1–2 tablespoons lemon curd

1 For the base, crush the biscuits into fine crumbs using a food processor or place them in a plastic bag and crush with a rolling pin.

2 Pour the crumbs into a bowl and mix them with the melted butter until evenly coated.

3 Press the mixture firmly into the base of 1 large ramekin or 2 small ones.

4 In a small bowl, beat the cream cheese, icing sugar and lemon juice with an electric mixer until smooth and creamy. Make sure not to overmix, as it can turn runny.

5 Scoop the mixture into the ramekin(s) and smooth it out evenly.

6 Spoon the lemon curd on the top of the cheesecake and smooth it out gently.

7 Refrigerate for at least 1 hour for best results.

8 You can store the cheesecake in an airtight container in the refrigerator for up to 3 days if you're not eating it immediately.

TIP

Feel free to decorate with a slice or two of fresh lemon.

Speculoos Cornflake Bars

Crispy cornflakes coated in white chocolate and Biscoff spread.
They're crunchy, chocolatey and so incredibly moreish.

INGREDIENTS:

60g (2¼oz) salted butter

30g (1oz) golden syrup or honey

210g (7½oz) Biscoff spread

340g (11¾oz) white chocolate,
   broken into small chunks

120g (4¼oz) cornflakes

1 Line a 20cm (8 inch) square tin with baking paper.

2 In a large saucepan over low heat, melt the butter with the golden syrup and 160g (5¾oz) of the Biscoff spread, stirring continuously until smooth. Don't overheat or it may split and turn lumpy.

3 Turn the heat down to the lowest setting, then add 190g (6½oz) of the white chocolate and stir until melted (again don't overheat).

4 Remove from the heat, then add the cornflakes to the mixture and stir until fully coated.

5 Tip the mixture into your lined tin and press down firmly with the back of a spoon to create an even layer.

6 Melt the remaining Biscoff spread and the remaining white chocolate in 2 separate bowls in the microwave on medium heat in 30 second bursts, stirring each time until smooth.

7 Pour the white chocolate over the cornflake mixture, followed by the Biscoff spread, then swirl them together with a skewer or knife to create a marbled effect.

8 Chill in the refrigerator for at least 1–2 hours or until set, then slice into 16 squares.

9 Store in an airtight container in the refrigerator for up to 5 days.

White Chocolate Hazelnut Biscuit Bars

This is a quick and easy recipe you can just throw together and it always turns out amazing! The soft, chewy, biscuity slice is packed with chunks of Kinder Bueno and topped with white chocolate.

INGREDIENTS:

350g (12oz) digestive biscuits

300g (10½oz) sweetened
    condensed milk

115g (4oz) salted butter, melted

10 Kinder Bueno bars, broken
    into 40 chunks

250g (9oz) white chocolate

1 Line a 20cm (8 inch) square tin with baking paper.

2 Crush the biscuits into fine crumbs using a food processor or place them in a plastic bag and crush with a rolling pin.

3 Pour the crumbs into a bowl and mix them with the condensed milk and 100g (3½oz) of the melted butter until evenly coated.

4 Gently fold in 24 of the Kinder Bueno chunks, being careful not to crush them too much.

5 Scoop the mixture into your lined tin and press down evenly with the back of a spoon.

6 Melt the white chocolate and remaining butter together in the microwave on medium heat in 30 second bursts, stirring each time until smooth. Pour it over the biscuit base and smooth it out evenly.

7 Place the remaining 16 chunks of Kinder Bueno in a 4 x 4 grid formation on top, pressing them in gently.

8 Chill in the refrigerator for at least 4 hours or until set and the base is firm. Slice into 16 squares and enjoy!

9 Store in an airtight container in the refrigerator for up to 5 days.

Mini Easter Egg Cheesecakes

Mini cheesecakes topped with colourful chocolate eggs, perfect for Easter. They're sweet, creamy and crunchy, and so fun to make.

INGREDIENTS:

150g (5½oz) digestive biscuits
75g (2¾oz) butter, melted
700ml (1¼ pints) double cream, chilled
350g (12oz) cream cheese, at room temperature
120g (4¼oz) icing sugar
160g (5¾oz) Mini Eggs, crushed, plus extra to decorate

1 Line 9 holes of a muffin tin with muffin cases.

2 Crush the biscuits into fine crumbs using a food processor or place them in a plastic bag and crush with a rolling pin.

3 Pour the crumbs into a bowl and mix them with the melted butter until evenly coated.

4 Spoon the mixture evenly between the muffin cases and press down firmly to create flat bases.

5 In a large bowl, whip 450ml (16fl oz) of the cream until it forms stiff peaks.

6 In a large mixing bowl, beat the cream cheese and icing sugar until smooth. Be careful not to overmix, as this can cause the filling to become runny and prevent it from setting properly.

7 Gently fold in the whipped cream, then fold in the crushed Mini Eggs until evenly distributed.

8 Scoop the cheesecake mixture into the muffin cases, filling each one to the top, then smooth the tops with the back of a spoon. Chill in the refrigerator for 3 hours or until fully set.

9 Whip the remaining double cream to stiff peaks and transfer to a piping bag fitted with a star nozzle. Pipe a swirl of whipped cream on top of each cheesecake and decorate with extra Mini Eggs.

10 Store in an airtight container in the refrigerator for up to 3 days.

TIP

If you're not serving these immediately, decorate with the Mini Eggs just before serving to avoid colour bleeding.

Thick Italian-Style Hot Chocolate

This rich, velvety hot chocolate is thick enough to eat with a spoon. Pure chocolate heaven in a mug, it's perfect for the colder months.

INGREDIENTS:

360ml (12½fl oz) whole milk

1 tablespoon cornflour

2 tablespoons granulated sugar

1 tablespoon cocoa powder

100g (3½oz) dark chocolate, finely chopped

STAPLE INGREDIENTS:

Salt

1 In a small bowl, whisk together 120ml (3¾fl oz) of the milk and the cornflour until combined to make a cornflour 'slurry'.

2 Put the remaining milk in a medium saucepan with the sugar, cocoa powder and a pinch of salt, and whisk constantly on a medium heat until combined and steaming hot.

3 Turn off the heat, then add the chopped dark chocolate.

4 Stir the cornflour 'slurry', then pour it into the pan and continue stirring until the mixture thickens. It should coat the back of a spoon.

5 Pour into small glasses (it's very rich) and enjoy!

TIPS

Use chocolate with 70% cocoa solids if you can for a rich flavour.

Feel free to top with whipped cream, a light dusting of cocoa powder, mini marshmallows or all three.

Birthday Cake Fudge

This creamy fudge has birthday sprinkles mixed through it. Fun, colourful and perfect for celebrations or as a gift, it's so easy to make.

INGREDIENTS:

400g (14oz) can sweetened condensed milk
500g (1lb 2oz) white chocolate, chopped
2 teaspoons vanilla extract
60g (2¼oz) rainbow sprinkles, plus extra for topping

STAPLE INGREDIENTS:

Salt (optional)

1 Line a 20cm (8 inch) square tin with baking paper.

2 Put the condensed milk and white chocolate in a medium saucepan. Stir continuously on medium-low heat until fully melted and smooth.

3 Remove from the heat, then stir in the vanilla extract and a pinch of salt, if using.

4 Let the mixture cool for about 2 minutes, then gently fold in the sprinkles.

5 Pour the fudge into your prepared tin and smooth out the top. Scatter a few extra sprinkles over the surface and press them in lightly.

6 Chill in the refrigerator for at least 2 hours or until fully set, then slice into 2.5cm (1 inch) chunks with a sharp knife.

7 Store in an airtight container in the refrigerator for up to 1 week.

TIP

Try to find rainbow sprinkles that don't leach their colour when moist.

Serves 9 · Prep time: 15 minutes, plus chilling

Easy Classic Tiramisu

A simple version of the Italian classic that doesn't compromise on flavour.
Creamy, coffee-soaked and effortlessly impressive.

INGREDIENTS:

350ml (12fl oz) double cream, chilled
50g (1¾oz) icing sugar
200g (7oz) mascarpone cheese,
   at room temperature
150ml (5fl oz) cold espresso coffee
36 sponge fingers
Cocoa powder, for dusting

1   In a large bowl, whisk the cream, icing sugar and mascarpone to soft peaks.

2   Pour the cold espresso into a shallow dish. Quickly dip half the sponge fingers into the coffee, one at a time, and arrange them in a single layer across the bottom of a 20cm (8 inch) serving dish. Don't soak them otherwise they can go soggy.

3   Spread half the cream mixture evenly over the top.

4   Repeat the layers, finishing with the remaining cream, and smooth it out nice and evenly.

5   Cover and chill in the refrigerator for at least 4 hours (or overnight) to allow the flavours to come together.

6   Just before serving, dust generously with cocoa powder and serve chilled.

7   Store covered in the refrigerator for up to 2 days.

Chocolate Hazelnut Fingers

This fancy little dessert looks so impressive, but is incredibly easy to make. Just grab some sponge fingers and your favourite piping nozzle and have some fun decorating!

INGREDIENTS:

100ml (3½fl oz) milk

140g (5oz) chocolate hazelnut spread (I use Nutella)

100g (3½oz) cream cheese

10 sponge fingers

100g (3½oz) chopped roasted hazelnuts, plus extra for decorating (optional)

1   Heat the milk in the microwave or in a small pan until it's steaming hot, then add 40g (1½oz) of the chocolate hazelnut spread. Stir it into the milk until it's smooth, then let it cool to room temperature.

2   In a large bowl, mix the cream cheese with the remaining chocolate hazelnut spread until smooth. Keep 60g (2¼oz) of this cream cheese mixture to use now and put the rest in a piping bag fitted with a large star nozzle.

3   Spread a dollop of the chocolate cream cheese mixture on the back of 5 of the sponge fingers, then press another sponge finger on top of each to sandwich them together.

4   Spread a little more of the chocolate cream cheese mixture over the sides of each pair so the chopped hazelnuts will stick.

5   Dip the pairs of fingers in the chocolate milk mixture to coat (this will help the sponge fingers soften), then sprinkle all the sides sides with chopped roasted hazelnuts.

6   Place them on a plate and pipe a long swirl of cream cheese mixture on top of each. Sprinkle with more chopped hazelnuts if desired.

7   Best eaten on the day, but can be stored in an airtight container for up to 2 days.

TIP

Decorate with a few whole roasted hazelnuts if you like.

Brown Butter Toasted Marshmallow Crispies

Classic crispy squares made extra special with nutty brown butter and gooey toasted marshmallows. They're sweet, chewy, crispy and totally irresistible.

INGREDIENTS:

250g (9oz) large marshmallows

120g (4¼oz) salted butter

160g (5¾oz) puffed rice cereal

50g (1¾oz) mini marshmallows

1 Line a 20cm (8 inch) square tin with baking paper.

2 Put the large marshmallows in an ovenproof dish and place under a medium grill until they start to toast on top, then set aside.

3 Put the butter in a large saucepan over medium heat and stir occasionally as it melts. Once melted, it will start to foam and sizzle – keep stirring.

4 After a few minutes the foam will subside, and you'll be left with golden brown specks at the bottom. Next the butter will turn a deep golden colour. As soon as it reaches a rich amber, take it off the heat so it doesn't burn.

5 Add the toasted marshmallows to the pan and stir until melted. If they're struggling to melt, return the pan to a low heat until melted, then remove from the heat.

6 Pour in the puffed rice cereal and stir until fully coated, then stir in the mini marshmallows until evenly distributed.

7 Transfer to your lined tin and press down gently with the back of a wet spoon (this helps prevent it sticking).

8 Leave it to set at room temperature for 1 hour, then cut into 16 pieces.

9 Store in an airtight container for up to 4 days.

INDEX

apples: autumn harvest salad 56; cinnamon apple crumble 150

avocados: chicken avocado burrito 69; classic chunky guacamole 134; creamy avocado salad 57; creamy avocado toast 20; crunchy rainbow wrap 61; E.A.T. breakfast bagel 16; green goddess pasta 99; veggie burrito bowl 50

bacon: ultimate breakfast sandwich 23

bagel, E.A.T. breakfast 16

bananas: banoffee pie 186; brownie baked oats 27; moist banana bread 161

bang bang chicken skewers 114

banoffee pie 186

barbecue sauce: BBQ pulled pork sandwich 122; cheesy hunter's chicken pasta 92

BBQ pulled pork sandwich 122

beans: homemade baked beans 126; loaded chilli cheese fries 121; tomato & butter bean soup 49; veggie burrito bowl 50

beef: cheeseburger bowl 66; cheeseburger tacos 108; double smash cheeseburger 117; hoisin beef noodles 76; one-pot lasagne soup 91

birthday cake fudge 212

blackcurrant flapjacks, white chocolate 140

blondies, chocolate caramel 178

blueberries: blueberry cheesecake 200; blueberry cheesecake overnight oats 32; blueberry muffin baked oats 28; lemon blueberry yoghurt cake 158

bread: best ever grilled cheese 46; cheese & ham toastie dippers 62; fresh tomato baguette 142; garlic bread and pizza baguette 145; moist banana bread 161, see also toast

bread rolls/burger buns: BBQ pulled pork sandwich 122; crispy chicken

Caesar sandwich 45; double smash cheeseburger 117; ultimate breakfast sandwich 23; veggie breakfast bun 15

broccoli: cheesy broccoli bake 133; golden roasted vegetables 129; hot honey halloumi rice bowl 106; peanut butter noodles 95; soy-glazed salmon rice bowl 113; sticky teriyaki chicken rice bowl 102

burger sauce 109, 117

cakes: chocolate school cake 157; cookies & cream cake 174; lemon blueberry yoghurt cake 158; lemon drizzle loaf cake 154; peach upside down cake 177; Victoria sponge cake jars 153

carrots: golden roasted vegetables 129; peanut butter noodles 95

cauliflower: golden roasted vegetables 129

cheese: autumn harvest salad 56; best ever grilled cheese 46; cheese & ham toastie dippers 62; cheese & red pepper egg bites 19; cheeseburger bowl 66; cheeseburger tacos 108; cheesy broccoli bake 133; cheesy hunter's chicken pasta 92; cheesy mashed potato 129; cosy tuna pasta bake 88; creamy Cajun chicken pasta 96; crispy chicken tacos 109; crunchy rainbow wrap 61; double smash cheeseburger 117; E.A.T. breakfast bagel 16; fancy pizza toast 53; garlic bread & pizza baguette 145; garlic Parmesan chicken tenders 105; green goddess pasta 99; hot honey halloumi rice bowl 106; loaded chilli cheese fries 121; marry-me chicken pasta 72; one-pot lasagne soup 91; pizza salad 57; sun-dried tomato pasta 80; ultimate breakfast sandwich 23; ultimate mac 'n' cheese 83; veggie breakfast

bun 15, see also cream cheese

cheesecakes: best vanilla cheesecake 201; blueberry cheesecake 200; mini Easter egg cheesecakes 208; one-pot lemon cheesecake 203; ultimate chocolate cheesecake 196–7

chia seeds: raspberry ripple chia pudding 40

chicken: bang bang chicken skewers 114; cheesy hunter's chicken pasta 92; chicken avocado burrito 69; creamy Cajun chicken pasta 96; crispy chicken Caesar sandwich 45; crispy chicken tacos 109; garlic Parmesan chicken tenders 105; marry-me chicken pasta 72; Mexican-style chicken & sweetcorn soup 65; one-pan pesto gnocchi 75; sticky teriyaki chicken rice bowl 102; sweet chilli chicken wrap 54

chickpeas: crispy chickpea sweet potatoes 118

chocolate: chocolate button shortbread 149; chocolate caramel blondies 178; chocolate chip muffins 170; salted caramel granola 31; salted chocolate tart 189; thick Italian-style hot chocolate 211; ultimate chocolate cheesecake 196–7; white chocolate blackcurrant flapjacks 162; white chocolate hazelnut biscuit bars 207

chocolate hazelnut spread: chocolate hazelnut fingers 216; soft & chewy chocolate cookies 169

chocolate school cake 157

cinnamon apple crumble 150

coffee: easy classic tiramisu 215

cookies: seasonal sugar cookies 181; soft & chewy chocolate cookies 169

cookies & cream cake 174

cream: banoffee pie 186; lemon cream puffs 165; lemon tiramisu 185; salted chocolate tart 189

cream cheese: chocolate hazelnut fingers 216; cookies & cream cake 174;

mini Easter egg cheesecakes 208;
one-pot lemon cheesecake 203;
one-pot speculoos cheesecake 193;
peaches & cream Danishes 166;
salted caramel cheesecake bars 172;
ultimate chocolate cheesecake 196–7

digestive biscuits: banoffee pie 186;
best vanilla cheesecake 201; salted
chocolate tart 189; white chocolate
hazelnut biscuit bars 207

Easter egg cheesecakes, mini 208
E.A.T. breakfast bagel 16
eggs: cheese & red pepper egg bites 19;
E.A.T. breakfast bagel 16; ultimate
breakfast sandwich 23; veggie
breakfast bun 15
everything sauce 66

flapjacks, white chocolate blackcurrant
162
fudge, birthday cake 212

garlic bread & pizza baguette 145
garlic Parmesan chicken tenders 105
gnocchi, one-pan pesto 75
golden roasted vegetables 129
granola bars, nutty 24
guacamole, classic chunky 134

ham: cheese & ham toastie dippers 62
hash browns: veggie breakfast bun 15
hazelnut biscuit bars, white chocolate
207
hoisin beef noodles 76
honey: bang bang chicken skewers 114;
crispy chickpea sweet potatoes 118;
honey mustard vinaigrette 56;
soy-glazed salmon rice bowl 113;
speculoos cornflake bars 204;
sticky glazed meatballs 141; white
chocolate blackcurrant flapjacks 162
hummus: crunchy rainbow wrap 61

ice cream, no-churn pistachio 190

kale: crispy chickpea sweet potatoes 118

lemons: creamy avocado salad 57;
lemon blueberry yoghurt cake 158;
lemon butter prawn linguine 84;
lemon cream puffs 165; lemon drizzle
loaf cake 154; lemon tiramisu 185;
one-pot lemon cheesecake 203
lettuce: cheeseburger bowl 66;
cheeseburger tacos 108; creamy
avocado salad 57; crispy chicken
Caesar sandwich 45; pizza salad 57
limes: classic chunky guacamole 134;
homemade fresh salsa 135

mangoes: bliss smoothie bowl 35
marry-me chicken pasta 72
marshmallows: brown butter toasted
marshmallow crispies 219
meatballs: sticky glazed meatballs 141;
Sunday night spaghetti & meatballs
87, 141
Mexican-style chicken & sweetcorn
soup 65
muffins, chocolate chip 170

noodles: hoisin beef noodles 76;
peanut butter noodles 95
nutty granola bars 24

oats: blueberry cheesecake overnight
oats 32; blueberry muffin baked
oats 28; brownie baked oats 27;
everyday protein pancakes 39;
salted caramel granola 31; white
chocolate blackcurrant flapjacks 162
Oreo cookies: ultimate chocolate
cheesecake 196–7

pancakes, everyday protein 39
pasta: cheesy hunter's chicken pasta 92;
cosy tuna pasta bake 88; creamy
Cajun chicken pasta 96; green
goddess pasta 99; lemon butter
prawn linguine 84; one-pot lasagne
soup 91; sun-dried tomato pasta 80;
Sunday night spaghetti & meatballs 87;
tomato & basil sausage rigatoni 79;
ultimate mac 'n' cheese 83
peaches & cream Danishes 166

peanut butter noodles 95
peppers: cheese & red pepper egg
bites 19; creamy Cajun chicken
pasta 96; crispy chicken tacos 109;
crunchy rainbow wrap 61; golden
roasted vegetables 129; hot honey
halloumi rice bowl 106; Mexican-
style chicken & sweetcorn soup 65;
sweet chilli chicken wrap 54; veggie
burrito bowl 50
pesto gnocchi, one-pan 75
pineapple: BBQ pulled pork sandwich 122;
bliss smoothie bowl 35
pistachio ice cream, no-churn 190
pitta bread: pizza salad 57
pizza: fancy pizza toast 53; garlic bread
& pizza baguette 145; pizza salad 57
pork: BBQ pulled pork sandwich 122;
sticky glazed meatballs 141
potatoes: cheesy mashed potato 130;
loaded chilli cheese fries 121
prawns: lemon butter prawn linguine 84
puff pastry: lemon cream puffs 165; mini
caramelized onion sausage rolls 138;
peaches & cream Danishes 166

raspberries: raspberry crumble bars 173;
raspberry ripple chia pudding 40
red cabbage: crunchy rainbow wrap 61
rice: hot honey halloumi rice bowl 106;
soy-glazed salmon rice bowl 113;
sticky teriyaki chicken rice bowl 102;
veggie burrito bowl 50
rice cereal: brown butter toasted
marshmallow crispies 219

salads: autumn harvest salad 56;
creamy avocado salad 57
salmon: soy-glazed salmon rice bowl 113
salsa, homemade fresh 135
salted caramel cheesecake bars 194
salted caramel granola 31
salted chocolate tart 189
sausages: mini caramelized onion
sausage rolls 138; tomato & basil
sausage rigatoni 79; ultimate
breakfast sandwich 23
seasonal sugar cookies 181

shortbread biscuits: cheesecakes 200, 203

shortbread, chocolate button 149

six staple ingredients 9

soups: Mexican-style chicken & sweetcorn soup 65; one-pot lasagne soup 91; tomato & butter bean soup 49

speculoos cheesecake, one-pot 193

speculoos cornflake bars 204

speculoos French toast sticks 36

spinach: chicken avocado burrito 69; green goddess pasta 99; marry-me chicken pasta 72

sponge fingers: lemon tiramisu 185

Sunday night spaghetti & meatballs 87, 141

sweet potatoes: crispy chickpea sweet potatoes 118

sweetcorn: Mexican-style chicken & sweetcorn soup 65

tacos *see* wraps

tiramisu, easy classic 215

toast: creamy avocado toast 20; fancy pizza toast 53; speculoos French toast sticks 36

tomatoes: cheeseburger tacos 108; cheesy hunter's chicken pasta 92; classic chunky guacamole 135; cosy tuna pasta bake 88; E.A.T. breakfast bagel 16; fancy pizza toast 53; fresh tomato baguette 142; homemade fresh salsa 135; loaded chilli cheese fries 121; marry-me chicken pasta 72; Mexican-style chicken & sweetcorn soup 65; one-pot lasagne soup 91; pizza salad 57; sun-dried tomato pasta 80; Sunday night spaghetti & meatballs 87; tomato & basil sausage rigatoni 79; tomato & butter bean soup 49; veggie breakfast bun 15

tropical bliss smoothie bowl 35

tuna: cosy tuna pasta bake 88

vanilla cheesecake 201

veggie breakfast bun 15

Victoria sponge cake jars 153

walnuts: autumn harvest salad 56

white chocolate: everyday protein pancakes 39; white chocolate blackcurrant flapjacks 162; white chocolate hazelnut biscuit bars 207

wraps: cheeseburger tacos 108; chicken avocado burrito 69; crispy chicken tacos 109; crunchy rainbow wrap 61; easy air fryer tortilla chips 134; sweet chilli chicken wrap 54

yoghurt: bliss smoothie bowl 35; blueberry cheesecake overnight oats 32; blueberry muffin baked oats 28; cheese & red pepper egg bites 19; creamy avocado salad 57; creamy avocado toast 20; everyday protein pancakes 39; lemon blueberry yoghurt cake 158; raspberry ripple chia pudding 40

GLOSSARY OF UK/US TERMS

UK	US
baking paper	wax paper
baking tray	cookie sheet
beetroot	beets
bicarbonate of soda	baking soda
biscuit	cookie
cake tin	baking tin, cake pan
caster sugar	superfine sugar
chickpeas	garbanzo beans
clingfilm	plastic wrap
cocktail stick	toothpick
coriander (fresh)	cilantro
cornflour	cornstarch
digestive biscuits	Graham crackers
double cream	heavy cream
foil	aluminum foil

UK	US
frying pan	skillet
golden syrup	light corn syrup
grated	shredded
grill	broil/broiler
icing	frosting
icing sugar	confectioner's sugar
jam	preserve
jug	pitcher
kitchen paper	paper towel
minced meat	ground meat
natural yogurt	unflavoured yogurt
pastry	pie crust
pepper (green/red/yellow)	bell pepper

UK	US
piping bag	pastry bag
plain flour	all-purpose flour
rapeseed oil	canola oil
self-raising flour	self-rising flour
sieve/sift	strain
single cream	light cream or half and half
soured cream	sour cream
sponge fingers	ladyfingers
spring onion	scallion
stock	broth
tart	pie
tea towel	cloth kitchen towel
Tenderstem broccoli	broccolini
tomato purée	tomato paste

ACKNOWLEDGEMENTS

Honestly, I can't believe this is my 5th book. It still feels so surreal to be sat here writing this and to be given the opportunity to share recipes that I love so much with all of you. Never in a million years did I imagine that baking in my tiny kitchen and posting videos online would lead me here, holding another finished book in my hands.

There are so many parts that go into creating a cookbook, the writing, the testing (and the re-testing... and sometimes the eating far more than necessary in the name of 'research'), the photoshoots, the colours, the design, and the endless rounds of checks to make sure everything is as perfect as it can be. There's no way I could do this alone.

To my incredible audience, thank you for watching, liking, commenting, sharing, baking along, and for being the reason this is even possible. I will forever be grateful that you choose to be part of this journey with me.

To my husband Bernie, thank you for believing in me when my confidence occasionally packs its bags and leaves the building. Thank you for your love, patience, and for eating every test batch without complaint (mostly). I couldn't do this without you.

To my amazing publishing team, Kate, Jaz and Scarlet, thank you for trusting in my vision and putting so much passion and care into making this book the best it can be.

To Danielle, the amazing photographer, along with Ted and studio mascot Bear, thank you for bringing these pages to life and for making the photoshoots so fun. To Becks and her wonderful assistants for styling every crumb to perfection and making every dish look incredible, to Megan for sourcing props that I now desperately want to steal for my own kitchen, and to Celso and Jon for capturing all my best angles and making me feel so comfortable.

Thank you from the bottom of my heart.

Love, Eloise x

ABOUT THE AUTHOR

Eloise Head, founder of Fitwaffle, began sharing easy and delicious recipes on social media in 2020 after becoming a personal trainer and realising that being healthy doesn't have to mean giving up the food you love – even if you have a massive sweet tooth. When the pandemic put the nation into lockdown, Eloise decided to build a community of bakers and foodies by sharing recipes to inspire, promote balance, spread joy and bring people together through the love of delicious food.

Her brand Fitwaffle has 16 million followers across social media, and she has featured on TV (This Morning, Blue Peter), on the radio (Gaby Roslin, BBC Radio Wales) and in the press (*Women's Health, Metro, Daily Mail, Evening Standard, Cosmopolitan, Stylist, Insider*).

- Instagram.com/fitwafflekitchen
- Instagram.com/fitwaffle
- Tiktok.com/@fitwaffle
- Youtube.com/fitwafflekitchen
- Facebook.com/fitwaffle

hamlyn

First published in Great Britain in 2026 by Hamlyn,
an imprint of Octopus Publishing Group Ltd
Carmelite House
50 Victoria Embankment
London EC4Y 0DZ
www.octopusbooks.co.uk

An Hachette UK Company
www.hachette.co.uk

The authorized representative in the EEA is
Hachette Ireland, 8 Castlecourt Centre, Dublin 15,
D15 XTP3, Ireland (email: info@hbgi.ie)

Text copyright © Eloise Head 2026
Design and layout copyright ©
Octopus Publishing Group Ltd 2026
Food photography (pages 2, 8–9 and 12–218)
copyright © Danielle Wood 2026
Portrait photography (pages 5, 7, 10, 11 and 223)
copyright © Celso Marrero 2026

Distributed in the US by Hachette Book Group
1290 Avenue of the Americas, 4th and 5th Floors
New York, NY 10104

Distributed in Canada by Canadian Manda Group,
664 Annette St., Toronto, Ontario, Canada M6S 2C8

ISBN: 978-0-600-63993-0
eISBN: 978-0-600-63994-7

A CIP catalogue record for this book is available from the
British Library.

Printed and bound in China.

10 9 8 7 6 5 4 3 2 1

Publisher: Kate Fox
Art Director: Jaz Bahra
Editor: Scarlet Furness
Copy Editor: Jo Smith
Food Photographer: Danielle Wood
Portrait Photographer: Celso Marrero
Food Stylist: Becks Wilkinson
Props Stylist: Megan Thomson
Assistant Production Manager: Lisa Pinnell

Stock illustrations: Tymofii Malynovskyi, Hein Nouwens/iStock

Standard level spoon measurements are used in all recipes.
1 tablespoon = one 15ml spoon
1 teaspoon = one 5ml spoon

Both imperial and metric measurements have been given in all recipes.
Use one set of measurements only and not a mixture of both.

Eggs should be medium unless otherwise stated. The Department
of Health advises that eggs should not be consumed raw. This book
contains dishes made with raw or lightly cooked eggs. It is prudent
for more vulnerable people such as pregnant and nursing mothers,
the elderly, babies and young children to avoid uncooked or lightly
cooked dishes made with eggs. Once prepared these dishes should
be kept refrigerated and used promptly.

Milk should be full fat unless otherwise stated.

Fresh herbs should be used unless otherwise stated. If unavailable
use dried herbs as an alternative but halve the quantities stated.

Ovens should be preheated to the specific temperature – if using
a fan-assisted oven, follow manufacturer's instructions for adjusting
the time and the temperature.

All microwave information is based on a 900 watt oven. Follow
manufacturer's instructions for an oven with a different wattage.

Pepper should be freshly ground black pepper unless otherwise stated.

This book includes dishes made with nuts and nut derivatives.
It is advisable for customers with known allergic reactions to nuts
and nut derivatives and those who may be potentially vulnerable
to these allergies, such as babies and children with a family history
of allergies, to avoid dishes made with nuts and nut oils. It is also
prudent to check the labels of pre-prepared ingredients for the
possible inclusion of nut derivatives.

Vegetarians should look for the 'V' symbol on a cheese to ensure
it is made with vegetarian rennet.